D0801877

Penguin Monarchs

THE HOUSES OF WESSEX AND DENMARK

Athelstan	Tom Holland
Aethelred the Unready	Richard Abels
Cnut	Ryan Lavelle
Edward the Confessor	James Campbell

THE HOUSES OF NORMANDY, BLOIS AND ANJOU

William I	Marc Morris
William II	John Gillingham
Henry I	Edmund King
Stephen	Carl Watkins
Henry II	Richard Barber
Richard I	Thomas Asbridge
John	Nicholas Vincent

THE HOUSE OF PLANTAGENET

Henry III	Stephen Church
Edward I	Andy King
Edward II	Christopher Given-Wilson
Edward III	Jonathan Sumption
Richard II	Laura Ashe

THE HOUSES OF LANCASTER AND YORK

Henry IV	Catherine Nall
Henry V	Anne Curry
Henry VI	James Ross
Edward IV	A. J. Pollard
Edward V	Thomas Penn
Richard III	Rosemary Horrox

THE HOUSE OF TUDOR

Henry VII	Sean Cunningham
Henry VIII	John Guy
Edward VI	Stephen Alford
Mary I	John Edwards
Elizabeth I	Helen Castor

THE HOUSE OF STUART

James I	Thomas Cogswell
Charles I	Mark Kishlansky
[Cromwell	David Horspool]
Charles II	Clare Jackson
James II	David Womersley
William III & Mary II	Jonathan Keates
Anne	Richard Hewlings

THE HOUSE OF HANOVER

George I	Tim Blanning
George II	Norman Davies
George III	Amanda Foreman
George IV	Stella Tillyard
William IV	Roger Knight
Victoria	Jane Ridley

THE HOUSES OF SAXE-COBURG & GOTHA AND WINDSOR

Edward VII	Richard Davenport-Hines
George V	David Cannadine
Edward VIII	Piers Brendon
George VI	Philip Ziegler
Elizabeth II	Douglas Hurd

DOUGLAS HURD

Elizabeth II

The Steadfast

Elizabeth R

ALLEN LANE

an imprint of

PENGUIN BOOKS

ALLEN LANE

UK | USA | Canada | Ireland | Australia
India | New Zealand | South Africa

Allen Lane is part of the Penguin Random House group of companies
whose addresses can be found at global.penguinrandomhouse.com.

Penguin
Random House
UK

First published 2015

001

Copyright © Douglas Hurd, 2015

The moral right of the author has been asserted
Cover artwork: *Balmoral (Queen Elizabeth II in the 1970s)*, 2002, by Elizabeth
Peyton. Monotype with handpainting on Twinrocker handmade paper,
30 × 22 inches (76.2 × 55.9 cm). Copyright © Elizabeth Peyton.
Published by Two Palms, NY.

John Betjeman, 'Death of King George V' from *Collected Poems* © The Estate of John Betjeman
1955, 1958, 1960, 1962, 1964, 1968, 1970, 1979, 1981, 1982, 2001.
Reproduced by permission of John Murray Press,
an imprint of Hodder and Stoughton Limited.

Set in 9.5/13.5 pt Sabon LT Std
Typeset by Jouve (UK), Milton Keynes
Printed in Great Britain by Clays Ltd, St Ives plc

ISBN: 978-0-141-97941-0

www.greenpenguin.co.uk

Contents

Preface

Over the last ninety years, the world has changed more rapidly than at any time in history. When my grandmother the Queen was born in 1926, the wounds of the Great War were still healing, but few would imagine how soon they would be reopened. The confidence of the previous century had morphed into uncertainty and many worried – as they still do – about the challenge presented to our communities by rapid technological and social change.

After almost ninety years, we find ourselves in a world that has changed dramatically, almost beyond recognition from the world that the Queen was born into, but where the role of charity, family, duty and compassion perseveres. I think I speak for my generation when I say that the example and continuity provided by the Queen is not only very rare among leaders but a great source of pride and reassurance. Time and again, quietly and modestly, the Queen has shown us all that we can confidently embrace the future without compromising the things that are important.

From a personal point of view, I am privileged to witness the private side of the Queen, as a grandmother and great-grandmother. The Queen's kindness and sense of humour, her innate sense of calm and perspective, and her love of family and home are all attributes I experience first-hand. I should add that no mention of the Queen is complete without paying tribute to my grandfather Prince Philip, who has devoted his life to supporting her.

All of us who will inherit the legacy of my grandmother's reign and generation need to do all we can to celebrate and learn from her story. Speaking for myself, I am privileged to have the Queen as a model for a life of service to the public.

HRH Prince William, Duke of Cambridge, 2015

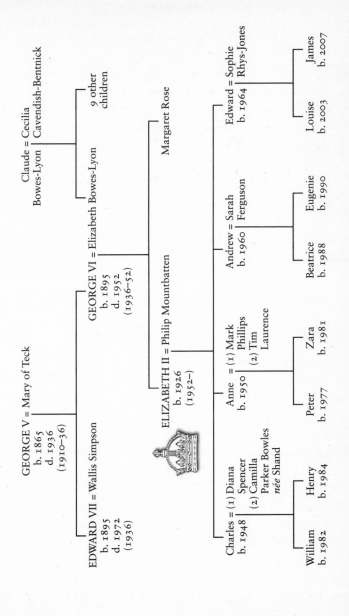

Claude = Cecilia
Bowes-Lyon Cavendish-Bentinck

GEORGE V = Mary of Teck
b. 1865
d. 1936
(1910–36)

9 other
children

EDWARD VII = Wallis Simpson
b. 1895
d. 1972
(1936)

GEORGE VI = Elizabeth Bowes-Lyon
b. 1895
d. 1952
(1936–52)

Margaret Rose

ELIZABETH II = Philip Mountbatten
b. 1926
(1952–)

Charles = (1) Diana
b. 1948   Spencer
(2) Camilla
Parker Bowles
née Shand

Anne = (1) Mark
b. 1950   Phillips
(2) Tim
Laurence

Andrew = Sarah
b. 1960   Ferguson

Edward = Sophie
b. 1964   Rhys-Jones

William
b. 1982

Henry
b. 1984

Peter
b. 1977

Zara
b. 1981

Beatrice
b. 1988

Eugenie
b. 1990

Louise
b. 2003

James
b. 2007

Elizabeth II

I
Lilibet

The Minister of State was ill at ease. He had only been in the job for three weeks and did not know how the message he carried would be received. The Queen was busy writing at her desk; she glanced up as he approached. 'A message from the King of Morocco's Chamberlain,' the Minister said. 'The King has changed his plan for this evening: he is now going to sleep at Fez instead of Casablanca, and asks if you could very kindly change the time of your dinner on *Britannia* so that it starts at 10 p.m. instead of 9 p.m.' 'I see'; the Queen returned to her writing, then called her Private Secretary. She discussed with him the details of that day's programme. The Minister of State stood, shifting from one foot to the other, conscious that on the deck outside the King's Chamberlain was waiting for a response.

Having had time to reflect, the Queen gave her reply: 'Please explain to the King that unfortunately we cannot alter the time of tonight's dinner because at least fifty people have been invited at the earlier time. But I shall entirely understand if the King arrives a little late.'

And so it was. The King of Morocco reached the Royal Yacht more than an hour late in a thoroughly bad temper, accompanied by three princes who had not been invited to the dinner. The Queen and Prince Philip coaxed the King back into a sunny mood and by the next morning, the last of this state visit, the atmosphere was all sunshine, smiles and the exchange of gifts.

This was the first and the stormiest of my overseas expeditions with Her Majesty. In her company, I visited Russia, France, the United States, South Africa – and the Channel Islands. On shore as Home Secretary I took part in several royal ceremonies. Each bishop of the Church of England has to take an oath of allegiance to the Queen, kneeling on a footstool in front of her, with the Home Secretary in attendance. A venturesome bishop once suggested to me that the time had come to bring this oath up to date, for example by removing reference to the Bishop of Rome as a person having no jurisdiction in this our realm of England. I took careful note of his suggestion, thought about it, and concluded that such a change would bring hornets buzzing around my head from several directions. I thanked the bishop; no action was taken. So far as I know that sleeping dog sleeps on.

Several years later, as Foreign Secretary, I was quite often brought into company with the Queen. These occasions were by their nature fleeting. The Queen is a very private person and I certainly would not claim any privileged access to her thoughts or inner feelings, nor am I qualified to produce a definitive account of the constitutional significance of her reign. There will be others who will feel able to venture yet again on the details of the Queen's family life, and others who can analyse her reign as part of the long evolution of the British monarchy. This book is rather an attempt to blend those two approaches – to describe something of the Queen's reign as it appeared to one of her ministers, and tentatively to offer some thoughts for the future.

Elizabeth (known as Lilibet to relations and close friends) is the elder daughter of Albert George, the second son of King George V. Albert George owed his first name to his great-grandmother, Queen Victoria, whose determined devotion to the memory of her husband ensured that his name was carried on through several generations. But Albert George preferred and more often used his second name and throughout his life he was generally known as Prince George, or by close friends as Bertie. He took the title of Duke of York. The Duke was good-looking, conscientious and dutiful in obedience to his father, the King. Like his father, he had joined the Royal Navy and took part at the age of twenty-one in the Battle of Jutland, the only major engagement of the First World War between the Royal Navy and the German High Seas Fleet.

After the First World War the Duke retreated into the shadows. He became known for organizing the Duke of York's summer camps for boys of different backgrounds. These were a success, but he left most royal duties to his brother Edward, the Prince of Wales, who basked in the glamour of his good looks and determined pursuit of upper-class pleasures. Only once did Bertie divert the limelight from his elder brother, when he courted and, after being twice refused, was accepted by Elizabeth Bowes-Lyon, daughter of the Earl of Strathmore, a leading Scottish aristocrat. His bride was, in the parlance of the day, a 'commoner', in whose veins no royal blood could be detected. But no one could cavil convincingly at his choice of the beautiful and charming daughter of a long-established Scottish peer. To those in the know (a much smaller number than the frenzied spectators of royalty today), the real defect within the Royal Family lay with the Duke of York himself, pleasant and dutiful though he was. The duties of a Royal duke, then as now, consisted mainly of making public speeches. Bertie suffered from the crippling burden of a severe stammer; he hated speaking in public for fear of breaking down, as he almost did in 1925 when he struggled to complete a speech at the Empire Exhibition at Wembley. Bertie, powerfully supported by his wife, fought to conquer his stammer; the story was well told in the 2010 film *The King's Speech*, which details how he called on the services of an Australian therapist, Lionel Logue. The treatment was painful but gradually it worked. Bertie emerged as a reasonably impressive public speaker.

But for the British public, during the inter-war years, the Duke of York's future lay in providing help and support for his brother, the Prince of Wales. Edward, a fluent speaker, outshone his brother in every important respect except one: Edward so far had no wife and therefore no heir, but that was a gap which could yet be filled without too much difficulty. The Prince of Wales was only in his thirties and had shown himself formidably attractive to women. True, the ladies whom he attracted were mostly already married, but that was surely a habit that could be broken. Therefore there was nothing feverish about the public reaction to the birth of Princess Elizabeth on 21 April 1926. A small crowd gathered outside the house in Mayfair where the Duchess of York went into labour, but they were waiting for the arrival of a royal princess rather than a future queen.

One of the first experiences of the new baby was to be introduced to her grandfather, George V. This proved a great success; the old King had been stern and sometimes harsh to his own children, but to the new arrival he soon unbent. She came to call him 'Grandpa England', and to the amazement of his courtiers he played games with her on the nursery floor and waved to her from the balcony of Buckingham Palace. George V is regarded nowadays as having been a staunch conservative and rather stuffy, associated in the public mind with traditional values and a prolific stamp collection, but he was the first king to work with a Labour Prime Minister and in 1917 he changed the name of his family, getting rid of the German title (which had been Saxe-Coburg-Gotha) and substituting it simply with 'Windsor'. Elizabeth's grandmother, Queen Mary, outwardly severe but inwardly warm, also played a major part in the Princess's upbringing.

In 1930 Elizabeth was joined by a baby sister, Margaret Rose. The two Princesses saw their parents often and grew up in a close-knit family atmosphere. Indeed the family regarded itself as a team of four facing the world together. A central figure in the lives of the two Princesses at this time was a Scottish teacher, Marion Crawford, who was their governess from 1933 to 1948. Marion Crawford later spoiled her reputation by writing a book about her work.

Read today, the greatest surprise about *The Little Princesses* is that the book should have caused quite such a stir. Marion Crawford's account of her daily life with the Princesses is blandly discreet compared with the outpourings that have marked some later publications about the Royal Family. Crawford's book was shocking not because it was the worst of its kind, but because it was the first. The British public had not yet learned to enjoy gossip about a Royal Family, which in those early days still commanded respect and, in general, silence. Marion Crawford paid the price for her indiscretion: she was condemned to banishment from the royal world. No one from the Royal Family attended her funeral in 1988. In spite of her disgrace, however, we can now see that Marion Crawford did a good professional job, and the two Princesses grew up to do her credit.

While Margaret revealed a streak of mischief which made her the favourite of her father, Elizabeth from a young age showed herself obedient and accepting. Elizabeth's great steadiness was perhaps first challenged when several changes of fortune came on each other's heels in the mid 1930s. In 1935, King George V celebrated his Silver Jubilee and discovered that he was admired, even loved, by most of his people. But within a year, at the age of seventy-one, he had died, and his place was taken by his eldest son. In his poem 'The Death of King George V', Betjeman signalled something of the meaning of the loss of the old King – staunch, stalwart, a countryman – and the breathless arrival of the new King, by air, into an airport at the edge of an ever-sprawling city:

The big blue eyes are shut which saw wrong clothing
And favourite fields and coverts from a horse;
Old men in country houses hear clocks ticking
Over thick carpets with a deadened force;

Old men who never cheated, never doubted,
Communicated monthly, sit and stare
At the new suburb stretched beyond the runway
Where a young man lands hatless from the air.

Elizabeth was still too young to grasp fully the implica-
tions of the abdication crisis of 1936. It is doubtful whether
she heard her parents discuss the rapid turn of events
which transformed both their futures and her own. To
Princess Elizabeth, Edward VIII was a young bachelor
uncle who used to come and play with her and Margaret
but stopped doing so when Grandpa England died and he
became King. Later she simply said that she and Margaret
had called him Uncle David, and that he had always
remembered her birthday. This was a time of whispered
rumours and speculations which were decidedly not for
the ears of children. By his own actions, Edward VIII
renounced the throne. He proved weak and feckless in
almost all his dealings as a monarch, but on the central
issue he was as firm as a rock: he would not take his father's
place on the throne without Wallis Simpson at his side
as Queen, to which the Archbishop of Canterbury, the
Cabinet and the Prime Minister, Stanley Baldwin, were
wholly opposed. To them she was divorced, and that was
that. Edward's only important supporter was Winston

Churchill, but to most people this was an old man past his prime and his pleas on behalf of the King were received in chilly silence.

The abdication was prepared and Edward explained himself to the British public in a dignified broadcast on 11 December 1936. Listening to this broadcast in 2015, we have to wonder whether if it were made today it would fall on such deaf ears. The nation is more broad-minded than in 1936, and there might be a powerful reaction in favour of Edward's commitment above all else to 'the woman I love'. But at the time the view of the nation was clear and the abdication went ahead. We exchanged a gifted but foolish King for his brother, who after a tremulous start, earned a sure place in the hearts of the nation. He was to be the last British Emperor of India and the first Head of the Commonwealth.

Elizabeth would not have shared the despair of her father, who was abruptly proclaimed as King George VI and ushered into a world for which he believed himself wholly unsuited. She did not know that he had wept bitter tears in front of his mother, Queen Mary, nor would she have been aware of the resentment of her own mother, who felt that her husband's life had been shattered (and later shortened) by the selfishness of his brother and Mrs Wallis Simpson. For Princess Elizabeth and her sister, the main and unwelcome effect of the abdication was that they had to leave their comfortable home at Royal Lodge in the middle of Windsor Great Park, and move into the very different world of Buckingham Palace, which no one has ever regarded as a home. 'For ever?' Elizabeth asked Marion Crawford; 'Yes of course,' came the reply. The same day the Princesses practised their curtsey to their father when, as King, he came home to lunch. The governess spent the first night at the Palace listening to the wind moaning in the chimneys and woke up feeling homesick for her old Scottish life. The change confronting Elizabeth was more formidable. Princess Margaret asked her sister if it meant that one day she would be Queen. 'Yes,' she replied, 'I suppose it does.'

It was the Coronation of George VI in May 1937 which opened Elizabeth's eyes to the reality of her new life. She wrote an account of the ceremony for her parents, in simple, straightforward prose. After enthusing about the sandwiches and orangeade (she was eleven years old), she concluded that the whole event was 'very wonderful, very wonderful'. A new element soon entered Elizabeth's education. Earlier there had been press reports that she would be sent to a boarding school, but the idea had been rejected by the old King, and this decision was ratified by Edward during his short reign. The choice of a school would cause jealousy among other schools; how could Elizabeth be protected from unsuitable schoolmates; would she have to study extra subjects in addition to those taken by other girls? These objections may not look decisive to us today but they were enough for George V and his son, Edward VIII. So Elizabeth never went to school and instead, before long, two names were added to the list of those who called regularly on the family.

A skilful tutor, the Vicomtesse de Bellaigue, was found to teach the two girls French, which Elizabeth at first found difficult but later exploited to excellent effect on several expeditions to France. The contrast between the fluency of the Queen in French and the stumbling efforts of some of her ministers has been noticed in France: it is one reason for the admiration and affection which she has earned in dealing with that most difficult people. A more testing addition to the Queen's education was provided by Sir Henry Marten, the Vice-Provost of Eton College, who lived across the Thames from Windsor. Marten was cautious and conservative by instinct. Elizabeth enjoyed history and took trouble with it. Sir Henry's task was to bridge the gap between the reality of Britain in 1939 and the history books that Elizabeth was advised to read. Wisely he concentrated on two themes – the development of the Commonwealth following the Statute of Westminster of 1931 and the importance of broadcasting. Both these themes were accepted without question by Elizabeth and both added something important to the way in which she interpreted her duties.

This was the heyday of the Boy Scout movement and the Girl Guides. The two Princesses were both girl guides and a special company was formed for them at the Palace, made up of the carefully selected daughters of their parents' friends and other vetted acquaintances. They met on Wednesday afternoons and as a group they absorbed the movement's message of cheerful dutifulness. There are no stories of rebellious daughters battling against the teaching handed down to them. Princess Margaret developed a defiant streak in later life. The Queen, by contrast, was by nature an accepting person and she took in without question or dissent the information and advice which she was given.

While their contacts in the Girl Guides were perfectly friendly, what the two girls lacked was the freedom of unfettered friendships with children of their own age. Sir Henry Marten, the Vicomtesse and Marion Crawford did their best but there remained other social and cultural gaps which were hard to fill. Where were the musicians who could open their ears to the enchantment of music? Where were the artists who could open their eyes to the beauty and significance of pictures, not least those in the Royal Collection? This last was a field in which the British monarchy was expected to show a lively and knowledgeable interest. Although, of course, previous British monarchs had often failed this test, and the ones who most clearly passed it (Charles I and George IV) are not counted among our more successful sovereigns.

Once it became clear that Princess Elizabeth was certain to succeed her father on the throne, something more specific had to be done to prepare her for that destiny. Her parents always faced a difficult choice; they were anxious not to lose the atmosphere of a happy and unpretentious family which as Duke and Duchess of York they had deliberately created. The two sisters, Elizabeth and Margaret Rose, as she was then called, had no political experience or interests. They were simply agreeable representatives of the English upper class.

Elizabeth's life was about to change radically thanks to a good-looking young man, Prince Philip of Greece. He was Elizabeth's distant cousin: they had a common great-great-grandmother, Queen Victoria. Philip came from a divided and unhappy family and in early life was tossed about Europe from school to school. Philip's mother, Princess Alice, suffered from serious mental illness and spent the formative years of his childhood in a Swiss sanatorium. Her father, Prince Andrew of Greece, took a pivotal part in the civil wars of that country. He and his family were evacuated in December 1922 from Corfu by a British warship, HMS *Calypso*, at the behest of George V. Without strong parental support – he saw little of his mother beyond the age of ten – Prince Philip was advised and helped by his uncle, Lord Louis Mountbatten. Mountbatten was tireless in backing whatever idea captured the Prince's enthusiasm of the moment, a trait which was both to help and hinder his nephew in the years ahead.

In 1939 Philip was asked to look after the two Princesses when they visited the Royal Naval Academy in Dartmouth. Philip was eighteen, a boisterous cadet, very handsome and full of fun. Their first meeting had probably occurred at the Duke of Kent's wedding in 1934 and again at the Coronation of George VI in 1937. These were formal royal occasions to which Philip and Elizabeth were invited as members of the Royal Family but they were too young to attract each other's attention. In the few years following their meeting in 1939, though they were often separated, Elizabeth did not forget Philip; indeed she fell in love with him. Philip was reserved about his own emotions but he too was in love. He proposed and was accepted, but had to wait until 1947. The King's assent to the marriage was required and he gave it on the condition that the engagement should not be announced until Elizabeth and her parents had returned from a long-planned visit to South Africa. The King and his wife were not hostile to the wedding, but thought that their daughter needed time to be sure of her own mind.

2

Princess in Uniform

The Second World War began a new chapter in the training of the two Princesses. They were of an age (Elizabeth was thirteen in 1939 and Margaret was nine) to understand that something phenomenal was happening: the British nation was struggling for its life. Patterns of behaviour which they had taken for granted suddenly had to change. Small acts of self-denial were progressively elevated into rules laid down by law and enforced by pressure of public opinion. The curtains had to be drawn tight at night so that no chink of light could reach the Luftwaffe which was always deemed to be overhead. A black line in a bathroom at Buckingham Palace marked the level within which guests of the King and Queen, and their own daughters, were expected to limit their indulgence in hot water. The two Princesses learned to dig for victory in the Palace gardens. Actions big and small which had previously been personal and a matter of taste became matters of patriotic duty.

Elizabeth and her sister found themselves acting as models and standard-bearers for their contemporaries in Britain and the Commonwealth. The spread of radio across the world meant that the way they behaved was studied and commented on overseas, most keenly in the United States.

As the Duke of York's daughters they had been of small account; as the daughters of the King their doings became famous internationally. There was no downside to the story of the teenage girls playing a small but noticeable part in the cause of Britain's lonely stand against the Nazis. Elizabeth thrived in this atmosphere; she followed the rules and pressed her father to allow her a more active role. She gladly put on the uniform of the Auxiliary Territorial Service (ATS), the women's branch of the British Army. Thanks to the ATS Elizabeth learned about the inner workings of a motor car. On Victory in Europe Day in 1945 the girls were allowed to wander through the crowds and enjoy the general rejoicing.

The royal tour of South Africa, for which the engagement of Elizabeth and Philip had to wait, took place in early 1947. This was the first time that either Princess had set foot abroad. The South African Prime Minister, Field Marshal Smuts, was particularly keen on the visit, which was connected, in his mind at least, with bolstering his (unsuccessful) campaign to be re-elected. The royal visit went well, despite the hostility of part of the Afrikaner press. On her twenty-first birthday – 21 April 1947 – Elizabeth broadcast from South Africa to the British Empire. In the high voice of someone who had not long emerged from childhood she dedicated her whole life, 'whether it be long or short', to serving the people of the Empire.

Elizabeth and Philip's engagement was announced on 9 July 1947. They were married on 20 November that year in Westminster Abbey. Her parents had also been married in the Abbey, but there was no established tradition to that effect. Earlier royal marriages had been held in different and less glorious places. The choice of the Abbey conveyed a message of celebration to a weary British public beset and impoverished by years of austerity and rationing, which lasted in Britain longer than in most other Allied countries. The Labour government under Clement Attlee was keen to show the public that life could be fun. They were relatively forbearing about the expense despite the misgivings of Hugh Dalton, the Chancellor of the Exchequer. The wedding was a family as well as a state affair, and among those present were the representatives of foreign princes and princesses. Princess Margaret noted that 'people who had been starving in little garrets all across Europe suddenly reappeared'. The media fastened happily on details of the wedding cake and of course the wedding dress. On the day itself, large crowds lined the route of the procession, establishing a tradition which with few exceptions has remained solid ever since; the number of people turning up was greater than the experts had predicted.

Elizabeth spent much of the first part of her married life with Philip as he returned to his career as a naval officer. Inevitably she stood out to some extent, since everyone in Malta – where Philip was stationed in 1949 – knew she was the King's daughter. The difference between her and the other officers' wives was emphasized by the presence in Malta of Lord Mountbatten, who relentlessly thrust the young couple into the company of admirals. But Elizabeth had plenty of time for riding and for the company of her husband. To our modern eye it may seem odd that she decided to leave her baby son Charles in London.

He had been born in November 1948 and was well looked after, but not by either of his parents. There was no suggestion of neglect in this separation; it was simply the custom of the time.

The cheerfulness of these days in Malta was overshadowed by the King's illness. George VI was not an easy patient. He was increasingly subject to spells of bad temper which his children called his gnashes. The Queen and her daughters defended him and themselves with the belief that the King was on the way to recovery, but this argument wore thin as the months passed and his doctors grew increasingly gloomy. The King and Queen had to abandon their plans for a visit to Australia and New Zealand in 1949; in 1951 he was diagnosed with lung cancer. It was agreed that Elizabeth and Philip should carry out the first stage of the Dominion tour by visiting Kenya, still at that time a British colony. They said goodbye to Elizabeth's parents on 31 January 1952. A few days later, after a happy day's shooting at Sandringham, King George dined with his wife and younger daughter. He went up to bed, and died in his sleep. The news was flashed to Kenya and reached Elizabeth and Philip at Sagana Lodge near Treetops, the famous point from which wildlife could be watched. The new Queen and her husband walked in the garden in deep conversation. Although she had been devoted to her father, the Queen did not break down or show any strong emotion. She apologized to those around her for spoiling the rest of their visit to Kenya. The discretion and self-containment shown in those few hours of silent grief have set the tone for the whole of her reign.

3
A Monarch for Modern Times

Back in London Elizabeth was received at the airport by Winston Churchill, the Prime Minister, along with the Leader of the Opposition and other senior political figures, all wearing black. The suddenness of the King's death took the general public – who had not realized that his life was in such danger – by surprise. The outstanding image of these days is a photograph of the three Queens, Mary and the two Elizabeths, standing side by side in deep mourning. That evening the Prime Minister broadcast to the nation using words which showed loyal sorrow and his abiding sense of English history. I remember as an undergraduate listening to him from my Cambridge college; I wrote down his closing words, which seemed (and still seem) memorable: 'I, who spent my youth amid the august, unchallenged and tranquil glories of the Victorian era, may feel a thrill to raise again the prayer and the anthem,' (then rather loud) 'God Save the Queen.'

During the Queen's reign her subjects have lived through a commotion of change. Our children's and grandchildren's lives are almost unrecognizable to us, their predecessors. Only in the reign of Queen Victoria was the pace of change so hectic, and the differences in terms of human experience so striking. Queen Victoria's far-flung subjects had witnessed the climax of the Industrial Revolution, which briefly propelled Britain into the leading position in the world. These changes brought both improvement and deterioration. In both eras the standard of living for most people was greatly enhanced and they lived longer. The innovations of Victoria's reign, including the spread of railway travel, the use of electricity and modern methods of dealing with illness and sewage, transformed the lives of millions of British citizens. On the negative side, millions of people moved from villages into stinking and disease-ridden cities. The expansion of world trade brought to the British shopper a range of consumer goods previously unimaginable except for the small minority of the rich. This progress has continued unabated during the reign of Elizabeth II. The spread of television has transformed the way in which most citizens spend their hours of leisure; and millions of people have been able to explore the world thanks to the growth of mass air travel. The creation of the welfare state meant that illness and old age carried far lighter penalties than in the past.

It is futile to try to balance out the good and the bad during these two long reigns. In neither of them was the influence of the Crown determining. But the decisions and behaviour of both monarchs were clearly affected by the ups and downs of national life. Queen Victoria ruled a country which, by hard work and good fortune, had created for itself a dominant position, resisted by some but not successfully challenged on the battlefields between the victories at Waterloo and El Alamein. Both were expensive victories, but victories all the same.

Queen Elizabeth II, having served in the Second World War, watched how the world's statesmen, including her own, tried but failed to construct a lasting peace. She has reigned over a country which was still paying the price of the huge sacrifices in what is rightly called the Great War, and the lesser sacrifices of the Second World War. Both monarchs lived long enough to drive through the cheering streets of London to celebrate their Diamond Jubilees; but Elizabeth has reigned over a very different country from that of her great-great-grandmother. Elizabeth is Queen of a country which, though still capable of great things, has lost that sense of unchallenged superiority which Victoria enjoyed. That loss has made necessary a different style of monarchy. The Queen knows very well that her subjects have a dual view of their monarch. On the one hand they wish her to keep and use the trappings of monarchy. They would not relish the pedestrian and undramatic style of her Scandinavian and Dutch counterparts. Elizabeth's subjects expect to see the crown and the glitter of royal diamonds on suitable occasions. They rejoice with the Queen on her royal birthday and the anniversaries of her succession. They expect men and women of undoubted gallantry and long public service to be honoured by the Queen or by members of her family. But at the same time they expect the Queen to keep the monarchy up to date. This requires a difficult blend of skills. They expect the Queen to move but not to be seen moving. In his masterpiece *The Leopard*, Giuseppe di Lampedusa remarks that

1. Princess Elizabeth with her family in the garden of their home at Royal Lodge, Windsor, in 1936, unaware that in a few months' time her uncle, Edward VIII, would abdicate and her father would become King George VI.

2. An active role: Elizabeth as a 2nd Subaltern in the Auxiliary Territorial Service, April 1945.

3. Cape Town, 21 April 1947: Elizabeth about to make her twenty-first birthday speech to the British Empire, during which she pledged to dedicate her life to its people.

4. Princess Elizabeth and Prince Philip, the new Duke of Edinburgh, after their wedding ceremony in Westminster Abbey on 20 November 1947.

5. The new Queen comes home: returning to London from Kenya on the news of her father's death, 7 February 1952. She was greeted by (left to right) Lord Woolton, Anthony Eden, Clement Attlee and Winston Churchill.

6. Three Queens in deep mourning: Queen Elizabeth II, Queen Mary and Queen Elizabeth, the Queen Mother at George VI's funeral, St George's Chapel, Windsor, 15 February 1952.

7. Queen Elizabeth II at her Coronation in Westminster Abbey, 2 June 1953.

8. The Queen's traditional Christmas broadcast to her people and those of the Commonwealth is a much-loved part of Christmas.

9. With five former and one serving Prime Minister, 10 Downing Street, December 1985: (left to right) James Callaghan, Alec Douglas-Home, Margaret Thatcher, Harold Macmillan, Harold Wilson and Edward Heath.

10. Trooping the Colour, June 1986: the Queen rides her horse Burmese for the last time.

11. Elizabeth II working on her red box of official papers, 1991.

12. The Queen is welcomed off the Royal Yacht *Britannia* by Isa bin Salman Al Khalifa, the Emir of Bahrain, during her tour of the Gulf States, 14 February 1979.

13. A rare show of emotion: with Prince Charles and the Duke of Edinburgh at the decommissioning service for *Britannia*, 11 December 1997.

14. *Annus horribilis*: surveying the damage caused by the fire inside Windsor Castle, 21 November 1992.

15. The Queen and the Duke of Edinburgh among the well-wishers and floral tributes outside Buckingham Palace on the eve of the funeral of Diana, Princess of Wales, 5 September 1997.

16. Sheer enjoyment: the Queen watches one of her horses compete in the Veteran Horse class at the Royal Windsor Horse Show, 11 May 2011.

17. 'Your Majesty – Mummy': Prince Charles pays tribute to the Queen as she joins performers on stage at the end of the Diamond Jubilee Concert at Buckingham Palace, 4 June 2012.

'if we want things to stay as they are, they must all change'. That has been the paradox the Queen has had to negotiate across her reign.

The Queen is by nature shy. She does not usually laugh out loud, though she keeps in reserve for private occasions a deep laugh which she must have inherited from one of her Hanoverian ancestors. She knows that in repose her face can look disapproving or even sullen; she has cultivated a smile which is neither forced nor condescending.

She has to think carefully about the occasions on which, year by year, she is expected to speak in public. As a girl her voice was high and somewhat thin. Her natural caution means that she prefers to speak from a written script which she can practise in advance. This greatly reduces the risk of stumbling into a mistake. Over time, her voice has become deeper and, to most of her audience, more natural. However, unlike Prince Philip and the Prince of Wales, she sees little merit in the spontaneity which brightens up their speeches but from time to time has landed both of them in trouble.

One regular event badly needs amendment. The Speech from the Throne delivered by the Queen at the opening of each parliamentary session is painful to hear and must be even more difficult to deliver. Just about everyone knows that she has had no involvement in its composition. It is the fruit of deliberate consultation among her ministers. The resulting document has none of the natural form and harmony of the English language. The search for compromises between ministers often produces a mess and a muddle. Sometimes ministers, unsure of themselves on some detail, use a deliberately ambiguous form of words which the Queen is expected to deliver as if it has some meaning. A possible remedy is to hand: I believe that the Queen's Speech to Parliament should be the work of one minister only, in partnership with the Queen. Every Cabinet still produces at least one minister who knows how to use the English language to good effect. The Prime Minister should designate one, but only one, of his or her colleagues for this task, which should count as a chore but also a privilege.

The Queen's Christmas broadcast is another regular event and was invented by the Queen's grandfather, George V; it is a much-loved part of the nation's Christmas routine that should continue unchanged. The Queen might, however, be encouraged to include in it more by way of personal experience and reflection. It is a unique occasion for the Queen to communicate directly with her people and those of the Commonwealth. She and her advisers can be a little bolder in their choice of words and subjects without losing the political neutrality which lies at the heart of our monarchy.

4
Political Pitfalls

It is more difficult to maintain this political neutrality than is generally supposed. It is a path littered with snares, big and small. There is a relationship between the Queen's words in her Christmas broadcast and on other public occasions, and popular opinion as a whole. In Britain, as elsewhere, popular opinion has its vagaries. It can be powerfully influenced by events which are impossible to predict in advance. This has always been the case, as every prime minister knows. Prime ministers can help to shape opinion by their own efforts, but they are sometimes caught napping. Disraeli, for example, was surprised by the effect on opinion of Gladstone's pamphlet of 1876 in which he denounced the atrocities committed by the Turkish authorities on their Christian subjects in the Balkans. Disraeli misjudged the public reaction and had to work hard to turn opinion back to accept the traditional British policy of protecting the Ottoman Empire. The prime minister can influence opinion, as Disraeli then did, in the direction which he or she wants. It was not long before public opinion once again agreed with his view on the threat from Russia.

Much later, Margaret Thatcher had little success in

persuading public opinion to accept the poll tax. Tony Blair fared little better in lining up opinion to support the war against Iraq in 2003. On the other side of the ledger, prime ministers led Britain to victory in two World Wars without any serious popular opposition. Victoria gave Disraeli full and strong public backing in a way impossible to imagine today, but since her time the Crown has weakened its influence on policy. By underlining its political neutrality, the Crown in the twentieth century in effect renounced the right to decide or even to influence the policy of the Queen's ministers. The great nineteenth-century writer on the constitution, Walter Bagehot, had in 1867 listed the right to warn ministers of the dangers of a particular policy as one of the monarch's functions. Until the archives of her reign are opened we shall not know what, if any, use the Queen has made of the 'right to warn'. Her natural caution indicates that she will have used it sparingly, by asking questions rather than assuming answers.

This raises an important question about the nature of the Queen's audiences with a prime minister. Do these conversations consist (as I suspect) mainly of a general explanation of government policy by the prime minister? Or is the Queen in the habit of cross-examining her prime minister about particular proposals and, if she thinks fit, of warning about what she might see as the likely consequences? We can ask these questions but need not wait for an answer. A veil of secrecy descends, for we are tiptoeing close to the secret inner workings of our constitution.

Bagehot did not specify how the Crown should exercise

the duty of warning. The question arose in a very practical form at the time of the Suez Crisis of 1956–7. We shall probably never know how, if at all, the Queen made her feelings known on the Crisis, which so divided the nation and inflamed parliamentary discussion. We do know that the Queen was disturbed to find that her own staff were also divided and sent them an informal message that they should try to sort out their differences before talking to her. By this time Winston Churchill had resigned as Prime Minister and been succeeded by Anthony Eden. The Queen quickly agreed to Eden's request for a general election, at which he and the Conservatives won handsomely. The Queen saw Eden every week and was on excellent terms with him. The letters which they exchanged after his retirement in January 1957 have been published and were remarkably friendly; the Queen would not have sent these letters if she thought that Eden had just been lying to her and concealing his determination to get rid of President Nasser by force.

How open and complete were the Prime Minister's dealings with her during those weeks when the military action was being planned to depose Nasser and install a less hostile Egyptian government? The Queen did not rely only on her Prime Minister for her knowledge of government policy. She was sent intelligence material from all three of our intelligence agencies, MI5, MI6 and GCHQ. Their reports did not pile up unread in a corner of Buckingham Palace. The Queen is a faithful reader with an exceptionally retentive memory.

There were several layers of deceit on Eden's part. I

think it likely that the Queen knew about the government's intention to use force against Egypt. She would have been aware from her other sources that military action was being planned. She might well have accepted that the preparation and the decision to use force had to be concealed from public and Parliament. I do not suppose that Eden lied to the Queen, as he had lied to the House of Commons; there had probably been no need to do so. That Britain's Prime Minister was determined to bring down Colonel Nasser, if necessary by using force, was quite widely known and would have been supported by about half the British people. The real blot on his reputation was the fact, which he continued to deny, that he intended to act in collusion with the French and the Israelis. The collusion was not revealed in any of the documents which the Queen had seen; we cannot tell how he would have answered a direct question as to whether he was in such a conspiracy, dressed up to appear as an attempt to keep the peace. On this issue the Queen was not directly lied to because she did not cross-examine her Prime Minister on the detail of the operation. Indeed there was no particular reason why she should act as a prosecuting counsel against her Prime Minister. The Prime Minister had told her in strict confidence that he was planning to use force against a man whom he and most of his colleagues judged to be an enemy of Britain. This was true; but it was not the whole truth.

After Eden's resignation in January 1957 there were two obvious candidates to succeed him as Prime Minister – Rab Butler and Harold Macmillan. Eden was not asked to give formal advice, which the Queen would have been obliged to accept, but he personally felt that Butler should be preferred: his general views on home affairs were similar to Eden's and Eden thought that he deserved the prize for his long record of public service, even though Butler had been a supporter of Chamberlain's appeasement policy in the 1930s. It was decided that an august individual capable of standing outside was needed to adjudicate the contest between the candidates for the premiership. The choice of umpire fell to Lord Salisbury, who in 1957 held the position of Leader of the House of Lords. The Queen's Private Secretary, Lord Adeane, telephoned Salisbury and suggested he take soundings of the Cabinet. Salisbury invited the Lord Chancellor, Lord Kilmuir, to join him in this task and these two men started the process of ascertaining opinion within the Conservative Party. They decided to confine this exercise to the Cabinet, but Lord Poole's opinion was sought as to the general feeling of the Conservative Party in the country, and Ted Heath as Chief Whip was similarly requested to report on opinion within the Conservative Parliamentary Party. Neither Poole nor Heath was asked to take soundings, but simply to give their personal view. The result was overwhelmingly in favour of Macmillan. The Queen was so informed and she sent for Macmillan, who duly formed a government which lasted until October 1963.

Since then the two main political parties have developed more democratic methods of choosing their leader. Nothing, however, has been done to define more closely the role of the Queen. There has been no attempt to remove or whittle away the Royal prerogative in the choice of a prime minister. The Queen's role as arbiter of an otherwise intractable constitutional choice is generally accepted. But some argue for a clearer definition of her role, and the historian and constitutional expert Professor Peter Hennessy has sketched his own well-informed idea of how this should be defined. He admits that the counter-argument against attempting such a definition is strong, but he was heartened by the appearance in 2011 of the Cabinet Manual, which throws light on how the Queen might be expected to handle the most likely difficulty of all, namely a hung Parliament. One agreed conclusion emerged from these discussions in the 1970s: the Queen will remain the arbiter in such situations but she will be influenced in her decision by what is described as the Golden Triangle, namely the Cabinet Secretary and the Private Secretaries to the Queen and to the Prime Minister. These three officials dislike the title of the Golden Triangle, arguing correctly that there is no statutory basis for it.

The Conservative Party was unhappy and divided as a result of the failure at Suez and, as it was, there was no disposition to argue against the Queen's choice of prime minister on that occasion, which had been arrived at in a completely informal way without any rules and procedures laid down in advance. The next potential crisis in this matter occurred in 1963 when, on medical advice, Harold Macmillan decided that he was too ill to continue as Prime Minister. There are several categories of decision which remain within the Queen's power, however cautiously she may handle them. I am not now thinking of the vast range of fundamental decisions which monarchs must take and which have never been finally abolished. Some are crucial to the future of our country and include the right to declare war or remove a prime minister. These great decisions are hidden in the clouds. Apart from the stray novelist who may be tempted to conjure up circumstances in which the monarch might take back these powers into occasional use, there is no realistic body of opinion which would favour such a leap back into the past. I am thinking instead of the decisions which the Queen may in practice influence, perhaps conclusively. The path to be trodden by the Queen is sometimes rocky. The method of choosing a prime minister is usually clear enough: the Queen sends for the man or woman who obviously commands the widest support in the House of Commons, for example by winning a general election. But sometimes the choice is not clear, as between different candidates for the premiership. For example there may be an upheaval within the winning party, leaving two candidates with broadly equal claims to the premiership. There is provision for the Queen to take advice in these circumstances; in particular she may seek advice from the retiring prime minister. But sometimes this move may complicate rather than resolve the problem. When this happens the only arbiter must be the Queen. This may to some look like a leap back into the past; but a constitutional monarchy exists in Britain. When, under our system, no solution seems practicable without an arbiter it would be quixotic to cast around for an alternative authority when the obvious choice, namely the Queen, is ready to hand.

Although in 1963 Harold Macmillan's poor health prevented him from continuing as Prime Minister, he was not
too ill to forego the opportunity of, in effect, choosing his
successor. The Queen visited him in hospital and formally
asked for advice. He replied by giving her the result of the
canvass conducted by Heath and Lord Salisbury of the
views held by Conservative Members of Parliament on a
successor; in those days they were the only people who
could take part in the election of the Party leader. Although
Macmillan had at the outset favoured Quintin Hogg for
the position, he changed his mind. He told the Queen that
in his view she should send for Sir Alec Douglas-Home, the
Foreign Secretary, and ask him to form a government.

It is argued by some that he should have explained to the
Queen the complicated background to this conclusion. In
terms of political standing and previous public service the
prize might have been awarded not to Sir Alec but to Rab
Butler. Some aspects of Harold Macmillan's advice to the
Queen were questionable; for example, there was a risk
that Sir Alec might find it impossible to form a government
if he was opposed by Butler's many supporters. There is
still a debate as to whether the Queen should have declined
to accept Macmillan's advice immediately, and asked him
to make a more thorough canvass of Conservative opinion.
But the atmosphere in the House of Commons and the
press was already feverish and the postponement of a decision by the Queen would have inflamed it further if she
appeared to favour Butler and snub Macmillan. Regardless
of the Queen's own opinion on the choice she would, by
delaying her decision, have precipitated a constitutional

crisis. We are not (yet) accustomed to a long-drawn-out process of forming a government: we expect it to happen without delay. As it turned out, Sir Alec was able to obtain the support of enough senior colleagues to form a reputable Cabinet including Rab Butler. Sir Alec held office until he called a general election in the autumn of 1964 – and Harold Macmillan continued to take an active part in politics for several years after his retirement as Prime Minister. After 1979 he watched quizzically the ups and downs of Margaret Thatcher's period in office.

5
Royal Reserve

It happens that I have been able, thanks to the vagaries of our political system, to watch at close quarters the way in which on the one hand the Queen and Prince Philip, and on the other hand Margaret and Denis Thatcher went about their task of meeting people. The two men shared a similar experience: each had to put aside his own personal ambitions for the sake of his wife's calling. The styles of each woman, however, in their innumerable social exchanges, were quite different.

Margaret Thatcher was always perfectly presented and rarely ill at ease, even in adversity. In the Soviet Union she was famous as the Iron Lady, in the United States as a symbol of world freedom. On most of her visits she was admired, in a few she was controversial. To travel with her was to board a roller-coaster whose ups and downs were almost impossible to predict. She normally spoke from a script but often deviated from the words agreed in advance with her advisers. It was these impromptu asides that usually made the headlines – and sometimes created difficulties. The Prime Minister was naturally talkative and always expected the conversation to remain under her own control. Sometimes I shared a platform with her;

my job was to nod approval of what she said however far-fetched that was. I had to refrain from making any comments of substance until such time as we were alone together.

Margaret Thatcher was always fluent (and sometimes overpowering) in conversation; the Queen, having started out with a leading question, expected her visitor to make the running in reply. The Prime Minister did not hesitate to concentrate exclusively on an individual who was of special political interest to her; the Queen spaced out her time evenly among her interlocutors. The experience of meeting the Queen was of a different character to that of meeting the Prime Minister. The Queen's natural reserve sometimes underlined the exceptional nature of the encounter. She was not grand in manner but you never forgot that she was the Queen. Only rarely would the Queen drop into colloquial conversation whereas the Prime Minister was always ready for an argument. The Queen listened carefully and stored the result away. The Prime Minister often seemed to be concentrating more on working out her next contribution to the discussion. People bustled away from the Prime Minister, eager to report the conversation to others. A conversation with the Queen was more likely to be saved up and recounted to grandchildren.

Prince Philip does not thrust into general discussion with his own advice on government policy or any controversial matter. What he discusses with the Queen when they are alone together is something they keep to themselves. Prince Philip carries some wounds from earlier battles with the Queen's advisers. We must remember that he was dropped almost alone into the life of a royal Court. He was heavily outnumbered by those in government and in the Court who instinctively resisted change. He was a distant relative of the Royal Family, but the mix of German blood and Greek forebears was not immediately appealing to the established advisers of the Queen. His ally at Court was his uncle Louis Mountbatten, but this was an alliance with a harsh downside. Mountbatten had risen fast, a little too fast, in the Navy and was regarded as a pushy upstart by admirals and long-standing courtiers; his record as the last Viceroy of India was also controversial.

Like Victoria, one of the first issues which the Queen had to resolve was the position of her Consort. Philip is at heart a modern-minded sailor, with a will of his own. He was catapulted into a world of stiff courtiers and traditional procedures with which he had little sympathy. Prince Albert, by contrast, took a strong interest in politics and diplomacy and exercised through Victoria a keen involvement in much of the work which came to his attention on its way to her. He was a wise man, sensitive to the views of others, and he gradually worked himself into the position of the Queen's adviser, particularly on foreign affairs. Philip has had no such interest; his concern is with the modern world and with scientific innovation. He has no strong political affiliation and in any case no British government would tolerate a repetition of the influence which Albert held until his death.

Philip, therefore, was a somewhat novel but salutary addition to the cohort of old-fashioned Englishmen who surrounded the Queen. Lord Mountbatten had been very active in persuading the press that Philip was at heart an Englishman and an admirable husband for the Queen. But even before the wedding, Philip began to realize that Mountbatten carried a burden of his own. As mentioned, he had stirred up jealousies among his fellow admirals. As Prime Minister, Churchill had helped him on his upward path but was later disillusioned by the speed with which the last Viceroy of India had hurried through the final chapter of the British Raj.

Mountbatten was an ambitious man: he battled hard to insert his own name into Philip's title. In 1952, the Cabinet was told that Mountbatten had on a recent social occasion at Broadlands given the impression that the title of the dynasty would henceforward incorporate Philip's name so that his family would carry the title Mountbatten-Windsor. This unwise boast reached the ears of Queen Mary, whose husband George V had himself carried through the change in the family name to Windsor in 1917. Churchill urged the Cabinet to follow Queen Mary's advice to keep the Windsor name and they agreed. We do not know what Philip said to the Queen in private on the matter but, whatever it was, it was of no avail. The Cabinet discussed the question and in 1952 decided firmly that the Queen should be advised to retain Windsor as the royal name. This seemed to be a straightforward success for the conservatives in defence of the Windsor title and a rebuke for Philip. He certainly regarded it as such and criticized the decision, which made him – as he put it – the only man in Europe who would not pass on his name to his children.

By 1959 the Queen had realized that the Cabinet's decision

had been too abrupt. Something was needed to pacify Philip. Harold Macmillan was Prime Minister at the time, but the Queen chose a moment when he was away on his celebrated African tour, leaving Rab Butler to hold the fort at home. The Queen told Butler that she felt the need for a further change to meet Philip's point. The Cabinet discussed the matter again in January 1960 and a compromise was reached. The 1952 'Windsor' decision was confirmed, but an extra flourish was added by which any descendant of the Queen and Philip who was not close enough to the Crown to receive a royal title would be entitled to use the name Mountbatten-Windsor. The Queen, who was heavily pregnant with Prince Andrew, told Butler that this compromise had lifted a great load from her mind. Prince Philip was content that in this roundabout way his name could be preserved, and Mountbatten had to stop badgering the Queen on the subject. Philip calculated that he and the Mountbattens should accept what they had got because they were not going to get any more.

The routine of Court life is by its ritualized nature somewhat dull and repetitive. The Queen enjoys being Queen, so this is less of a problem for her. But for Philip the monotony was sometimes overpowering. Perhaps as a result of this, he unintentionally acquired a reputation for tactless, even brutal remarks which, according to the press, caused offence. Such comments were often born out of the sheer tedium of events. Without meaning to hurt anyone, Philip launched into conversations designed to stir things up. He longed for something exceptional to happen, and sometimes took risks to achieve this. The Chinese were referred to as 'slitty-eyed' and the Hungarians were mocked for being too fat. Once I found myself next to Prince Philip examining the carvings of French victories on the Arc de Triomphe in Paris. At the time we were making slow progress in ratifying the EU Treaty of Maastricht. Inscribed on the arch was France's success at a battle in Maastricht: 'Got it up already I see,' he said. Luckily neither the *Sun* nor the *Daily Express* was in earshot. As the years passed these episodes became fewer and better understood, and Prince Philip was increasingly identified for what he is – the Queen's talented and devoted husband. The way in which, in his nineties, he carries out a heavy programme of his own, as well as accompanying the Queen, is testimony to his stalwart sense of loyalty, both to his wife and to the country which has adopted him, ultimately with such affection, and which has given him the stability his early life so lacked.

6
A Flower for the Queen

An entertaining book could be written about the relationship between British monarchs and their heirs. In the eighteenth century under the Hanoverian Georges, this relationship settled into steady antagonism, prolonged and occasionally vicious, between each King and each Prince of Wales. The mixture of frustrated ambition and personal dislike was a toxic concoction which entertained or exasperated the public. In an age when political cartoons were common and merciless, uninhibited rivalry between the King and the king-to-be seemed endemic to the British constitution. Maintaining reasonable relations between the King and his successor sometimes seemed to depend on their meeting as seldom as possible. William IV had few dealings with his niece, who succeeded him in 1837 as Queen Victoria. A century later another King's niece became Queen Elizabeth.

But the Queen, unlike her own mother, felt no resentment towards her uncle Edward VIII or his unsuitable wife. The relationship with the Duke and Duchess of Windsor was bound to be tricky, but to a large extent this had already been dealt with during the Second World War by Churchill and King George VI. The Queen remembered her Uncle David, now the Duke of Windsor, as a handsome man clinging to his youth, rooted in the taste and habits of the 1920s. But Uncle David did not forget her birthday and the Queen did not expect or wish for more. She saw no point in pursuing a feud with the ex-King and she was not among those who blamed him for her father's early death. Indeed she visited him in Paris a few days before he died.

Queen Victoria had accepted rather crossly the gradual ebb of political power from the monarchy. She never followed her uncle William IV in dismissing a prime minister, as he had done with Melbourne in 1834. On the other hand, Victoria's stance was a long way from the politically neutral one we take for granted today: she pursued, for example, a relentless public feud against Gladstone of a kind that would now be unthinkable.

As there was less power at stake for the Royal Family to argue about, it became easier to settle down into what most of us would regard as normal human relationships. As Queen Elizabeth's reign progressed, the frailties of such 'normal relationships' became more apparent and public. Mirroring wider social change, broken marriages became commonplace. Divorce remained a sadness, but was no longer a tragedy which marked the life of a man or woman for ever. The Queen accepted the divorce and remarriage of her eldest son. There would now, I suppose, be little objection to a marriage between Princess Margaret and Group Captain Peter Townsend. Times change and we change with them, as does the Queen. But the pace and extent of our changes are even now to some degree mediated by the behaviour of the Queen. The House of Windsor can no longer pride itself on setting a moral example to the nation; it is now a model not of absolute moral strictness but of charity and good sense. Day by day, year by year, the Queen has set a solid example of both these qualities.

In this book I do not wish to analyse, let alone judge, the disintegration of the marriage of the Prince of Wales to Princess Diana. But the fact of the divorce cannot wholly be ignored in a book about Elizabeth's reign, since in its aftermath the Queen found herself facing her moment of greatest crisis in her relationship with the British people. Diana, Princess of Wales was killed in a car crash in Paris on 31 August 1997. The sudden and massive tide of sympathy for the dead Princess showed signs of turning against the Queen and her advisers.

When the news broke, the Queen was on holiday at Balmoral in the Scottish Highlands without a press secretary or access to advice from her ministers. She had to take a series of quick decisions in the days that followed. The Queen's main concern was for her grandsons, William, aged fifteen, and Harry, twelve, who were with her in Scotland at the time. The Queen had to explain to the boys the extraordinary circumstances of their mother's death. There had never been any doubt about Diana's genuine love for the boys; this was made all the more poignant by the loss which they evidently suffered. The Queen might well have thought that her preoccupation as a grandmother with the two boys mourning their mother would be understood and accepted in those tragic days, but it was not to be. Public opinion focused overwhelmingly on the dead Princess. Not since the Prince Regent's daughter Charlotte died in 1817 had there been such outpouring of emotion over a royal death, yet that of Charlotte, long before the invention of television, could hardly have provoked such a reaction in the nation as a whole. The empty flagpole at Buckingham Palace acted for some as a provocation. In vain the courtiers explained that the Union Jack was not a suitable flag for a royal palace and that the Royal Standard was only flown over a building where the Queen was actually in residence. The absent Queen and the empty flagpole threatened to become the symbol of a Queen and a Royal Family which, so people thought, had never really liked Diana and were indifferent to her death.

At Balmoral the Queen found herself without her advisers and condemned to lag twenty-four hours behind public opinion. And no one could be sure which way public opinion, in such a heightened state, would turn next. There were some in the Royal Family who believed that the Queen should make no concessions to what they regarded as an irrational, almost hysterical, mood which would surely subside of its own accord once Diana's funeral was over. But that was not how the Queen had been brought up. She had been trained not to leap to conclusions but to listen to many voices and weigh up their advice carefully. She kept silent while the question was argued out in front of her.

It might have been possible to leave the notorious flagpole empty until her return to London, as planned, at the end of her holiday. But that would have been regarded as a slap in the face for the multitude of her subjects who were in genuine mourning for a Princess who, whatever her vagaries, had captured the public's heart. The decision about the flag became linked with other decisions that had to be made. Should the Queen return to London and should she broadcast to the British people, and indeed a global audience, about Diana's death? These were matters which only Elizabeth could decide. She grasped the nettle and decided to return to London, to arrange for the Union Jack to fly at half mast from Buckingham Palace and all public buildings, and to broadcast to her people.

The Queen arrived at Buckingham Palace on the afternoon of Friday, 5 September. This was a tense moment for her. A huge crowd was still gathered at the gates. But the dominant mood was of relief that the Queen had returned home. It was not an occasion for loud cheers but the mood of the moment was caught by a lady who handed the Queen a flower. When the Queen promised to put the flower with the others left in honour of Diana, the lady replied: 'Ma'am, this is for you.' That evening the Queen broadcast about her sadness at Diana's death. There was no dramatic phrasing, none of the exaggerated pathos which characterized the mood of those tense days. But in its formal way it was a genuine expression of grief. She was not and would never be someone who wept in public.

Diana's funeral in Westminster Abbey was organized with customary efficiency by the officials of the Court. It took place on 6 September 1997, and passed off well. The two Princes had decided that they would follow their father behind Diana's coffin. Lord Spencer in his farewell words to his sister made the headlines with phrases which were applauded in the Abbey and outside. His sentences about the education of the young Princes met the mood of the day, but have had no sequel. People were glad that he spoke as he did, but if there was a challenge in his words it was not taken up. Very few, on reflection, believed that the Earl or his family offered an alternative model for the upbringing of the Princes.

The run-up to Diana's funeral saw the greatest threat to the Queen's authority of her entire reign. Because the crisis originated within the Royal Family, the Queen was at first disconcerted by its spiralling public intensity. For a few days they lived in a whirlwind. Diana, while alive, had been a challenge because she represented a glamorous idea of modern monarchy, gathering around her worshippers all the misleading glitter of a mercurial modern media. As the years passed, the Queen and Diana would have found a way of working together. Had they had the time, Diana might have become an ally of the Queen, alert to every shift of fashion, always chic and always unpredictable and exciting.

7
Farewell *Britannia*

The Queen, as we have seen, is instinctively cautious. She has always insisted on speaking from a script even though some of her audiences longed for her to break away from what were often speeches of generalized goodwill without real substance. She usually took her Foreign Secretary on foreign visits, or a senior deputy, so that she could shunt over to him any questions which were in essence political. But she had one extraordinary advantage: wherever she spoke it was for the whole British nation without political preference or bias. Her very presence in a country was a message of greeting from Britain as a whole. Sometimes her speeches conveyed a message that was all the more powerful for being partly hidden. No one who was present when the Queen visited Dresden in October 1992 will forget the silence which enveloped the entire crowd in the square as the Queen left the Kreuzkirche. By contrast in the other German cities she visited, such as Leipzig, she was greeted with loud cheers. In Dresden she would at once have perceived her dilemma, and it would have been wrong if she had ventured an apology for the havoc which the Royal Air Force had inflicted on the city in February 1945. The Queen Mother had only just unveiled in London a statue to honour Sir Arthur 'Bomber' Harris, the main advocate and architect of the raid. The Queen at Dresden was not apologizing; she was recording her sorrow for the destruction and misery which had resulted for the city and its people. The Queen was binding up the wounds as only she could do on behalf of Britain.

Another of the Queen's visits which could have gone awry was the one to South Africa in March 1995. The memory of her government's opposition to sanctions against the apartheid regime of South Africa was still raw in people's minds. No one could predict with certainty how the African townships would react to the presence of the Queen in their midst. Yet it would have been absurd to leave out of the programme the places which had unhesitatingly voted for the African National Congress at their first democratic election in April 1994. The Queen persevered with the visit and converted it into a triumph. Out of the townships along the road to Port Elizabeth there poured a mass of enthusiastic children, emerging in their best clothes from the shacks which were their homes. They ran alongside the Queen's car shouting their welcome. The Queen had not been to South Africa for over forty years but older people still recalled her girlish voice during the royal visit of 1947 when she had solemnly pledged herself and her life to the service of her people.

On all such occasions there was a risk; any one of them could have gone badly wrong. The Queen, each time, knew the risk and accepted it. She did not choose to be accompanied by the razzmatazz of an American president. She is at physical risk on countless occasions and accepts this as part of her job. When congratulated on the coolness with which she dealt with the intruder Michael Fagan when he burst into her bedroom at Buckingham Palace in July 1982, she commented: 'You seem to forget that I spend most of my time conversing with complete strangers.' In Britain the Queen walks about a city careless of danger, in situations where she puts herself at real risk of attack. No American president would expose himself to such obvious peril. Of course there are precautions which we do not see, but the truth remains: the Queen has decided that to do her duty she must behave in ways which make her impossible to protect. She lives like this because that is the only way to do her job. We are so accustomed to watching the Queen, accompanied by a lady-in-waiting, walking through a crowd, at times pausing for a few words of conversation, never changing her pace, that we forget the risk she runs nearly every day of her life. This is not just true in Ireland or South Africa or other places where history has, in the past, stirred up bitter emotions.

I recall one expedition to France in the Queen's company. We were running a few minutes late and on our way south from Paris the car moved swiftly through a tunnel of poplars typical of a French road. A group of old ladies in black were gathered at a crossroad. They could only have caught a glimpse of the Queen as she passed, but it was enough to set off an excited exchange, audible to me in the car following behind: '*C'est la Reine! C'est la Reine!*' We were miles from anywhere and the ladies must have travelled a long way to that crossroad. Perhaps they came with poignant memories of their own – Winston Churchill, the German occupation, the war and the liberation of France under de Gaulle – a host of events which they had seen in their lifetimes and which were, somehow, acknowledged by the Queen with a fleeting smile and the wave of a royal hand.

The Queen, though not ostentatious, did not forget the tools of her trade. An evening programme on the Royal Yacht *Britannia* always ended with the Royal Marines Beating Retreat on the quayside by which she was moored, culminating in the National Anthem. The subliminal message varied from one tour to another. The visit to Russia in 1994 began in a low key in Moscow as the authorities wrestled with an unfamiliar problem, namely the right way to receive a Queen. The visit gathered pace as it progressed to St Petersburg. The Queen visited the tombs of the Tsars in St Petersburg, site of the Queen's unforgettable farewell as *Britannia* negotiated the crowded bridges of the Neva on her way back to open sea.

The most important single tool of the Queen's trade was the Royal Yacht. *Britannia* was special to the Queen because she and Prince Philip had together chosen her decoration and furnishings near the start of her reign. *Britannia* was not a grand or showy ship, but the Queen and Prince Philip made it their home in an intimate way that could not be matched by any of her splendid palaces on land. Successive governments on the whole handled their relationship with the Queen successfully, but the failure in 1997 to replace *Britannia* was a blunder. It had become clear for some time that *Britannia* was nearing the end of her working life. Either she could be refitted and given maybe another twenty years of service, or the Queen could be presented with a new *Britannia* which could be smaller than the original. The arguments swayed to and fro in Whitehall and in the Royal Navy. There was a bureaucratic problem which would not go away. The expenses of the old *Britannia* were carried on the Ministry of Defence vote as just one more warship. Money would be short in the next Parliament and the admirals would resent carrying on their books the £60 million which the new *Britannia* might cost. The problem came to a head at exactly the wrong time.

Windsor Castle had just been repaired and refitted after the fire of 1992. Under John Major's government, Peter Brooke, as Secretary of State for National Heritage, had undertaken that the cost for the work should be paid for by the taxpayer, but he had been unable to deliver his promise. The Queen, bruised by this reluctance, was not in a position where she could be seen to ask for a favour, let alone a yacht, from the government. In the general election campaign of 1997 the Labour Party found themselves in difficulty on public expenditure. They were tempted to promise great projects but hard-pressed to explain how the necessary money could be found. Tony Blair, Leader of the Opposition, hit on a neat formula designed to keep the critics at bay: 'I can tell you one thing we are <u>not</u> going to do; we will not spend £60 million on a new Royal Yacht.'

Tony Blair knew too much about politics to be anything other than respectful in his normal dealings with the Queen; but on this occasion the temptation to take a cheap trick proved too strong. His cry was taken up by others in the Labour Party. Neither Blair nor his cohorts knew much about *Britannia*, but as a target the combination of 'Royal' and 'Yacht' was too hard to resist. After a final ceremony of farewell in which the Queen was most unusually seen wiping tears from her eyes, *Britannia* was allocated a berth at Leith in the port of Edinburgh where to this day she serves as a modest attraction to tourists as well as a reminder of happier days. Hardly a voice was raised in her defence and the government went on to spend £700 million on the Millennium Dome.

Britannia's main task had been to carry the Queen and other members of her family on visits overseas. She performed this duty with admirable efficiency, linking the service to the Queen with the maritime tradition of Britain. She was available for other public purposes. In my direct experience she carried British businessmen to Mumbai to provide a fitting setting for the signature of contracts between India and British firms. She visited Kuwait with the Prince of Wales to draw attention to the merits of the government's programme of privatization. These, and other similar events, could have been carried out in a hotel on shore but this would not have been the same; *Britannia* provided a unique and dignified setting in which the link with the Queen offered that something extra which made it memorable.

As part of the commemoration of the anniversary of D-Day in 1994 the Queen travelled to France on *Britannia* and at one stage sailed between two lines of Allied warships drawn up in the English Channel, their crews on deck in impressive parade. As *Britannia* passed, each warship dropped a wreath of flowers into the sea to commemorate their dead. I stood next to President Wałęsa of Poland, who did not conceal his tears. In an emotional but dignified way this act of homage, as I suggested to the Prime Minister at that time, provided the best possible argument for commissioning a new *Britannia*. A nation can draw strength from its past by such events. It was not to be, and we are poorer as a result.

8
Vox Populi

It is now possible to measure scientifically the state of public opinion about the Queen and the monarchy. In earlier centuries the ebb and flow of royal popularity were gauged in a much more haphazard way. The public response to the main events involving the monarch was noted without being measured. There were two main means of judging this – the buzz of courtiers and later of the press, and loudest of all the people of London, originally known as the London mob. Since the days of the Plantagenets those on the throne were affected by the actions of the crowd, not least because it could make its presence heard and felt in the streets of the City and of Westminster. The royal reaction varied from reign to reign. Some, like Richard II, used their personal presence to humour and persuade those outside the Palace gates, at least until they had acquired enough power to overcome them. For the Stuarts, London was always a problem. Charles II decided that his last Parliament should meet not at Westminster but in Oxford. The Gordon Riots of 1780 and the demonstrations in favour of George IV's wife Caroline showed that the power of the mob was still strong, though volatile in its opinions. There was in London no Versailles to separate the ruling elite from the crowd. The Duke of Wellington had to protect himself: even the hero of Waterloo was vulnerable to a stone-throwing London crowd. However, once he was dead only his victories were remembered; the Duke's funeral in 1852 was one of the great public events of the century.

Disraeli had drawn comfort from his reception by the crowd when he was applauded and Gladstone booed in 1872 as they gave thanks in St Paul's for the recovery of the Prince of Wales from typhoid. Usually men had to rely on the taxi driver, the stationmaster or the daily charlady for their estimate of the public's view. But at last a way of measuring opinion was emerging; it was in the form of a general election punctuated by occasional by-elections. As the franchise gradually expanded general elections became more accurate as a measure of public opinion. This was a godsend for those in positions of responsibility who had been accustomed to rely on casual conversations and fleeting impressions for their opinion of the public mood.

By the time the Queen came to the throne in 1952, opinion polls were emerging which purported for the first time to measure public opinion accurately and comprehensively. The Queen's advisers used these techniques on her behalf, but it is hard to find examples of the Queen altering her view to align it more accurately with the findings of the polls. Their impression on her was less direct. She knows that her ministers, and especially the Prime Minister whom she sees every week, are politically influenced by the polls. She adds their opinions to the store of information which she accumulates in her own exceptional memory. She adds the impressions given by hundreds of individuals with whom she finds herself conversing every week. This store of information, constantly refreshed, offers her a view of public opinion which she knows constitutes a sign-post for the action, or inaction, of those in authority, including herself. She has to compare these impressions with existing practice and consider what, if any, changes should be made as regards her own behaviour. If public opinion is definite in favour of a particular course of action with which she agrees, how can she help it forward? If she disagrees as a result of information received from a myriad sources, how, if at all, can she express that disagreement to those around her? How is this to be reconciled with the requirement that she should be politically neutral?

We saw this technique at work in 2014 at the end of the Scottish referendum campaign. Of course the public were interested in the Queen's view. Of course she could not express a view while keeping her reputation for neutrality. It was nevertheless her judgement that something should be said. She solved the dilemma by quietly urging her Scottish subjects to think carefully before they voted and to come together in friendship after the vote. No one of good-will could accuse her of making a partisan statement; yet no one of sense could be in doubt about her views.

An earlier example of her dilemma was provided by Rhodesia, a former Crown Colony which drifted into a unilateral declaration of independence in 1965. Public opinion was sharply divided, particularly within the Conservative Party. One important factor was the loyalty which Rhodesians, particularly white Rhodesians, felt for the Crown. How far could the Queen use that loyalty to press Ian Smith to abandon the ruinous course on which he had embarked? Was it enough to hold to straightforward support for her government in the UK? (One reason why she got on well with the British Prime Minister at that time, Harold Wilson, was his willingness to talk through with her his problems and possible ways of handling them.) The Queen was anxious to help; at one stage she was willing to send out Lord Mountbatten to act on her behalf. This idea came to nothing because of doubts about the basis on which he would operate; but it showed willingness on her part to become involved.

The argument over Rhodesia was a prelude to a wider and deeper one over Britain's membership of the European Union. This dispute has dragged on through the Queen's reign and is far from over. It has become central to a wider argument about Britain's place in the world. The Queen has kept a resolute silence on the whole issue even though, or perhaps because, it has become the major controversy of her reign. Only once has she made a notable speech on the subject, when in 1972 she emphatically set out her government's case for British membership of the EU, which she described as a 'great achievement'.

After that speech, she has steadfastly declined to enter the argument. This has become one of the great silences of the century and the question is far from dying away. British governments of both parties have lurched to and fro, now hostile, now wobbling from one side to the other. The Queen has enjoyed several visits to EU countries, notably France and Germany. There must be many occasions when she has been urged to make a clearer commitment but she has remained silent. Fortunately no one in the EU has seriously suggested that the time has come for Britain to abandon the monarchy in favour of a presidential system. Not even the most devoted federalist has pushed the argument to that length. The Queen remains secure on her throne, and indeed the other main pillars of the National State remain in national hands. The Bank of England continues to issue our currency. The Chancellor of the Exchequer raises and lowers taxes as he and the British Cabinet decide. Britain enters, or declines to enter, foreign conflicts on the decision of the Cabinet and with the consent of the House of Commons. These factors must baffle Eurosceptics with their fixed ideas about the erosion of British sovereignty. They do not silence those who believe that we would be safer and more British outside the EU; the Palace remains quiet. The press cannot point to any signal of royal approval. On other matters there have been leaks, and the papers have professed (often wrongly) to reflect the Queen's private views. On Europe she is not only quiet; she imposes quiet on all around her. Following the Conservative win at the 2015 general election, Britain will now go to a referendum on the subject of British membership; we can expect this silence to continue. There will, in the heat of that contest, be invitations for the Queen to take part. Neither the Queen nor her successor is likely to yield to their pressure. She does not, I believe, see any conflict of interest between Europe and the Commonwealth. The main Commonwealth issues were settled during Ted Heath's negotiations long ago. The neutrality of the Crown on Europe is essential given the depth of division on the issue inside the UK. The Queen could stir up a whirlwind on the subject but she chooses not to do so.

9
Crown and Commonwealth

The future of the Commonwealth remains a separate sub-ject. The Queen is the Head of the Commonwealth and is also the Head of State of a number of Commonwealth countries, including the UK and Australia. These are formal points; more meaningful is the affection which the Com-monwealth arouses in many British people. Anthony Eden, when he was defending the government's lukewarm policy towards European integration, asserted that the great majority of overseas mail to and from his constituents in Stratford-upon-Avon came from the Dominions, Aus-tralia, Canada and New Zealand.

He used this as an argument against Britain deserting the Commonwealth and joining a united Europe. If you made that case today it would probably still be true. Lord Beaverbrook used a similar argument against European integration when he and the *Daily Express* campaigned unsuccessfully against closer ties with Europe. Such ties beyond a certain point looked to him like a betrayal of the natural instinct of the British people. We had planted settlers in these Dominions; their willingness to rally round to help us in two World Wars was, in the opinion of such people, the clinching argument. These were our kith and kin; it was to them that we should look in time of trouble.

This argument is still powerful today and it has gained support, so far as I can see, through the Royal Family and certainly with the Queen herself. She sees it as a factor in the argument, but not necessarily the decisive one. A glance at the Royal Family's diary of engagements shows part of the reason. The Commonwealth is much more than a collection of governments; indeed its essence is not intergovernmental. It comprises a large number of voluntary associations brought together by a shared, if distant, experience. Surgeons, doctors, lawyers, members of parliament and many other professions gather at regular intervals because of an episode somewhere in their past lives which links them with Britain and the British.

The recent entry into the Commonwealth of Mozambique and Rwanda, countries which had no such historic associations with Britain, eroded what until then had been a crucial connection between Commonwealth countries. There may in future be more such countries, including some surprising ones. Each entry of a country without historic links with Britain would weaken the Commonwealth by dilution of what had until recently been a common feature of all Commonwealth countries.

Some supporters of the Commonwealth push their argument too far. They dream of a Commonwealth united as a bloc by a joint approach to world problems. Such a dream was common among the vehement partisans of the Empire at the end of the nineteenth and beginning of the twentieth centuries; it has turned out to be a mirage. Two World

Wars were a misleading guide. The original white Dominions themselves took the lead before and after the two World Wars in asserting their right to an independent foreign policy. In this they were followed by the new Commonwealth, namely all those who entered after India proclaimed her independence in 1947.

The members of the Commonwealth today differ on just about every subject under the sun, beginning with climate change and the shape of any new international order. They will argue their case vociferously, perhaps using forensic skills they learned at the Inns of Court in Britain. They put their arguments with humour, and when they differ from the line taken by Britain they register their dissent with regret rather than anger. The EU aims at speaking with one voice in international questions; if it fails in that attempt it counts it as a failure. The Commonwealth does not aim so high; it will discuss and disagree, but up to a point try to find an idiom for the disagreement which will bring different sides closer. The Commonwealth will not always succeed in this aim, nor will the EU; but in influencing the tone and spirit of debate the Commonwealth approach has much to commend it. When people share the same jokes and the same memories, their arguments against each other lose their power to hurt.

The Commonwealth is a ramshackle edifice but its coping stone is the Queen. The Queen has used to the full her gifts of diplomacy. She has presided over each Heads of Government meeting in a way which commands respect. We British tend to take this element of her role as automatic and part of the job. It is indeed part of the job because she has made it so, following in her father's footsteps, but herself working out a personal method of presiding which is unique. At Commonwealth Heads of Government meetings she employs the same techniques as she uses at home. She uses political neutrality as a means of reaching agreement by questioning rather than as a weapon for combat. The Queen has established and maintains such a remarkable position among Commonwealth leaders because everyone knows she will not exploit it for British advantage.

The Queen did not attend the last Heads of Government meeting in Colombo in 2013. She asked the Prince of Wales to represent her and he handled the task with his own skills and aplomb. The Queen is not immortal and the Commonwealth will one day have to choose her successor as Head of the Commonwealth. This could not have been on the agenda at Colombo; it was however significant that the Prince of Wales by general consent did his job well, in particular when navigating what might have been a divisive question, namely the treatment meted out by the Sri Lankan host country to the defeated Tamil rebels. Neither the Queen's decision not to go, nor the way in which the Prince of Wales handled that responsibility, attracted critical attention. It was accepted that an elderly lady in her eighties was entitled to ask her son to undertake a long journey and a major conference on her behalf. It does not follow that the Prince would be accepted as the Head of the Commonwealth in succession to his mother. There is at present no rival candidate but the Commonwealth might decide to leave the post in abeyance. Nothing should be taken for granted, but as things stand the Prince of

Wales must be favourite for the job, which he would do very well.

The members of the Royal Family are frequent visitors to Commonwealth countries and several are personally involved in holding high office in the professional associations. They would be reluctant to see those associations disappear as the result of a decision by HMG to leave the Commonwealth. Her Majesty's present ministers show no signs whatever of such a move. Indeed the controversy within the Conservative Party on Europe, which has several chapters still to run, has given rise to a revival of interest in the Commonwealth. There are those who believe that Britain let the Commonwealth down during the long negotiations on British entry into the EU and should make amends. New Zealand butter, Caribbean sugar and other commodities feature in this list of supposed betrayal. Under close examination these objections lose reality. There were anxious discussions on both these and other Commonwealth issues during the talks in the EU on British entry, but the terms of British entry were generally accepted in the Commonwealth as reasonable. Certainly the terms were harsher than would have been available to Britain had she been negotiating a decade earlier than she did, before the Common Agricultural Policy had taken shape. But it is not usually sensible to suppose that history can be rewritten.

During the middle of the Queen's reign there were signs of growing republicanism, not so much in the United Kingdom as in the overseas Commonwealth. Commonwealth members in Asia and Africa were not involved because they had already chosen their future as republics. Some smaller colonies were too small and economically vulnerable to think of a future without the link with Britain. But that left the three old Dominions, Australia, Canada and New Zealand, all economically important, all linked to the Crown by traditional ties of loyalty. In all three countries those traditions had weakened as the British trade pattern had changed and other ties had become more important. Two of the three had understandable reasons in favour of keeping the Queen as the Head of State. For Canada, the strength of her regional ties with her immediate neighbour paradoxically works in favour of retaining the monarchy, as it is a sign that Canada is different from the United States: *Vive la difference* – the tide of republicanism in Canada has ebbed and flowed but has never been powerful enough to swamp the instinct to be different from the US. A similar sentiment has been at work in New Zealand, where it is strongly felt that the country should not rush to imitate Australia. For her part, Australia had begun to diverge quite markedly from Britain in several respects. She had abandoned the 'white Australia' policy which had in the past limited immigration from countries other than Britain. Her strategic interests have aligned her more closely with the United States than with Britain. A growing number of Australians began to think that the link with the British Crown prevented Australia from walking tall as an independent country. One particular event helped to crystallize that variety of reasons. As already recorded, William IV was the last British King to dismiss a prime minister. It was indeed a quirk of history that the only recent action of this kind has been taken in Australia on behalf of the Queen by Sir John Kerr, who had been chosen by the Australian government to be Governor-General. He held not only the powers possessed by the Queen in the UK but also those important powers which in the UK had lain dormant and unused since 1834. Among these was the right to dismiss a prime minister.

Sir John Kerr exercised this power by dismissing the Australian Prime Minister Gough Whitlam in 1975. This came as the climax of an argument between the Governor-General and the Prime Minister over the powers of the Governor of Queensland. The Queen, through her Press Office, made it clear she had not been consulted in advance of this matter and was not aware of the plan to sack the Prime Minister and force a general election. But it was inevitable that this dramatic event strengthened the hand of Australian republicans. The Australian Labour Party had already adopted the policy of moving towards an Australian republic. However, when the matter came to a referendum in 1999 there was a clear majority (55 per cent to 45 per cent) against the proposed change. For the first time in history the role of the monarch had been put to a popular vote – and had triumphed. Of course it was soon realized that the vote was less a vote for the monarchy than a vote against the particular form of republic suggested on the ballot paper, namely the indirect election of a president. But the royal victory was undeniable. It was noticed that the Queen had not given up her position in advance of the referendum. She remained clear throughout that the choice was for the people of Australia and she saw no reason why she should give up before they had made their decision. The popular choice, when it came, was firmly in her favour although the Queen and her family had preserved a strictly neutral position throughout. In Australia and elsewhere in the Commonwealth, the Queen had regained the popularity which had surrounded her Coronation and her first years on the throne.

The most difficult of all disagreements between the British government and the Commonwealth were not concerned with the terms of British entry into the EU but with policy towards South Africa. It was widely supposed that Margaret Thatcher as Prime Minister sympathized with the harsh apartheid regime which the nationalist government enforced after they had won the whites-only South African election of 1987. According to this view, Margaret Thatcher's stalwart opposition to sanctions implied indifference to the abuse of black human rights which was at the core of South Africa's domestic policy. This analysis of Margaret Thatcher was mistaken. True, she was offended by any attempt of outsiders to teach her lessons about the rights and wrongs of apartheid. True, she treated as hypocritical any claim by the United Nations to rebuke let alone penalize South Africa for preaching and practising apartheid. But there was a crucial distinction in the Prime Minister's mind between defending the right of South Africa to work out its own policies and believing that these policies could be made to work.

Mrs Thatcher did not believe that apartheid could work, or indeed survive, and she passed on this contrary view in private to any South African leaders whom she met. She disliked the policy, not on moral grounds but because in the long run it was not workable. President de Gaulle had a similar view of the French position in Algeria. Mrs Thatcher advised in private that Nelson Mandela should be released from detention, but she would not join in any public clamour to the same effect. Mandela was aware of these views; although he criticized Mrs Thatcher's stand on sanctions he never accused her of supporting apartheid, and was very conscious of her efforts on his behalf.

For her part the Queen could never have been happy with a government policy which ranged Britain sharply against the great majority of the Commonwealth including Australia, New Zealand and Canada. But did she know of the Prime Minister's opposition to a South Africa policy which she believed was unworkable? We cannot know because there is no record of any discussion between the Prime Minister and her Sovereign, but it would be almost inconceivable that the issue should not have been discussed between the two at their frequent meetings, or that the Queen was in some way mistaken about the Prime Minister's private views. There was probably no confrontation between them, for that was not the Queen's way. She would have preferred to tackle the issue with some tactful questioning; but I cannot believe that the Queen was left in doubt about her Prime Minister's approach.

The Queen's visit to Ireland in 2011 was a different matter. There was no argument between the United Kingdom and the government of the Irish Republic. The Anglo-Irish Agreement had acknowledged the right of the Republic to hold and express a view about the governance of Northern

Ireland, but not to assert a veto over British government policy on the matter. The Good Friday Agreement between the Northern Ireland parties had established the basis on which government could be shared between them. What was required of the Queen at the right moment was not new negotiation but a striking symbol as proof of reconciliation and healing. Timing was crucial – a visit too early could have reopened old wounds; a visit too late could have failed in its objective. The visit had to take place when the old wounds were still smarting but when there had been enough progress to make it likely that the Queen would be well received. The seemingly irreconcilable had to be reconciled. Those who had fought for Irish independence should be honoured but so also should those who had fallen in the Great War while fighting for the British Empire as part of the British Army.

In Ireland, symbols speak powerfully to contemporary political reality, so it was crucial that the symbols should be got right. The visit could have failed if the Queen had unwittingly struck a false note in anything she said, did or wore. Never, I suppose, had a state visit been so meticulously prepared. Luckily the Irish were as keen as the British that the visit should be a success and the Queen put in a faultless performance, even speaking in Irish in her opening speech. Those of us who have lived through the turbulent years of the Troubles in Northern Ireland were amazed at the completeness of her triumph.

10
Annus Horribilis

On 20 November 1992 Windsor Castle caught fire and burned for several hours. The Queen was later photographed poking somewhat forlornly among what looked like the ruins. Windsor Castle had not been insured and it was estimated that the work of repair would cost about £40 million. The British media are structured in such a way that after a major event they quickly begin to focus on one particular fact which is easily understood. The Queen had some months earlier asked for a report from the Lord Chamberlain, Lord Airlie, on the general question of whether she should begin to pay income tax and if so in what form. As usual in Britain the history of the subject turned out to be complicated, indeed confused. It was true that the Queen paid no income tax; this was a practice which had crept step by step into being in the reigns of her father and grandfather.

Once the unkind searchlight of the press began to play on this situation the tax exemption became indefensible. The inequity between the treatment of the Monarch and of her subjects was found to be intolerable. Lord Airlie and his colleagues had begun their work but not concluded it. The Windsor fire and the commotion which resulted caught them in a difficult position. Public discussion quickly turned to other matters which were thought to be relevant: why did the Queen need so many palaces? What possible reason could there be for the tax exemption? Some of these were ancient, smouldering questions which suddenly blazed into life. The underlying fact became clear to the critics: they thought that the Queen was middle-aged and married to a crosspatch of a husband. Between them they seemed unable to control the doings of their extravagant and dysfunctional family. The magic which had surrounded the Queen at the time of the Coronation had faded away. Journalists and editors continued to respect the Queen herself but did not feel bound to show any kind of reverence to her family or the courtiers who surrounded her.

Efforts of the Royal Family to ingratiate themselves with the media had been frustrated either by their own behaviour (the Prince and Princess of Wales both publicly aired the problems they had with each other) or their clumsiness, for example in the ill-advised television show *It's a Royal Knockout*. The Queen's first attempt at a counteroffensive was bold but dangerous. At the Guildhall on 24 November 1992 she borrowed from one of her correspondents a phrase which became famous; in a voice husky with cold she said: '1992 is not a year on which I shall look back with undiluted pleasure. In the words of one of my more sympathetic correspondents, it has turned out to be an *annus horribilis*.' The phrase captured the public imagination, partly because the Queen did not normally slip into Latin but mainly because the speech struck a new note. The quoted phrase came in the middle of a passage acknowledging that the monarchy, like other institutions in a free society, must be open to examination, but that this should nevertheless be gentle and understanding in tone. This acknowledgement of openness was the heart of the speech and I was surprised in the audience to hear the undoubted note of self-pity. Indeed at first I took the phrase to be a reference to the general state of the nation. We had after all just fallen out of the effort to stabilize the currencies of Europe and were struggling to ratify the Treaty of Maastricht. But in its context it became clear that the Queen was referring to her private regrets and anxieties. Her son and daughter-in-law were entering the final phase of an unhappy marriage. Her favourite house had been, with difficulty, rescued from the flames; her image was portrayed without any mercy in the cruel cartoons with which the producers of the TV series *Spitting Image* delighted to amuse the nation. The national prospect was bleak, however the Queen for once was not thinking of the nation but of her family and herself. The phrase came from a bruised spirit which had nevertheless not been broken. On the whole people were right to think of the Queen as a human being, subject to some of the ups and downs of human life.

That speech in the Guildhall marked a turning point. There was plenty of sadness ahead for the Queen as for any lady in her seventies: her mother had died in March 2002 and was mourned by the nation in a way which baffled those who had only recently foretold the gradual decay of the monarchy. The Queen's younger sister, to whom she was devoted, had died in February. This was perhaps the low point of the Queen's reign, but she soon had reasons for rejoicing. Although first she had to deal with the long-standing question of her taxation.

Through the many years of the British monarchy there has been an argument, sometimes flaring up, sometimes dormant, between the Crown and the Crown's advisers. Indeed Charles I actually reigned for eleven years without summoning any Parliament at all, raising money by means other than direct taxation. The tactic of ruling without Parliament was eventually frustrated by Acts of Parliament which directed that it should be summoned at intervals of not more than three years (later amended to seven years) and eventually settling down at five years. Parliament has established that in ordinary times we know in advance the date of the next general election because it is fixed by law. This latest change, made in 2011, remains of questionable use and may well be further challenged in future. Meanwhile a separate argument has been continued about the division between the monarch's own expenditure and the general expenses of his or her government. In 1760 George III settled this argument by the creation of the Civil List, which would be voted by Parliament and produce a fund from which the Crown would finance its own expenses, separate from the general expenses of government.

In return for the Civil List, the monarch hands over to the Treasury the entire revenue from the royal estates and properties. This reform, with occasional modifications, was the system which the Queen inherited when she came to the throne in 1952. The reform was necessary because the Civil List had failed to keep up with the expenses of the monarch. The deficit in the monarch's own income was to some extent offset by transferring some royal responsibilities to the government. But there was a limit to this and by 1992 the limit had been reached. The Queen asked Lord Airlie to look at the whole scheme of royal financing and make recommendations. He was a good choice. David Airlie was a Scottish peer who owned a couple of Scottish castles and was widely known as a successful banker before that profession fell into disrepute. He was generally respected both by the Queen and by everyone else concerned with the negotiation which ensued.

One of Lord Airlie's first acts was to recruit expert help from the accountancy profession. He was joined by Michael Peat, who swept through the entire Royal Household in six months. This being Britain, there was no outward sign of internal tension; but within the Palace strong feelings were aroused as arrangements apparently sanctified by time were examined, found wanting and swept away. As usual on such occasions the emotions aroused bore no relation to the sums of money involved. The Ascot Office, which organizes the vetting of those admitted to the Royal Enclosure during the racing in June, was traditionally placed in St James's Palace. This was convenient for and agreeable to distinguished people such as the Queen Mother, but it was a financially nightmarish arrangement because it tied up highly valuable space to administer a meeting that occurred in one week a year. There were other examples of arrangements giving special treatment to senior members of staff which may have been defensible in the nineteenth century but could have no place as we moved towards the twenty-first. The Royal Box at the Albert Hall was another such example, so were the dining rooms at which, in a carefully graded sequence, members of the Household took their luncheon. The aim of this exercise was of course to stop the haemorrhage of resources out of royal spending. In 1991/1992, before Airlie and Peat began work, the whole royal expenditure was £65.5 million; by 2000 that cost was down to £38 million. This was in sharp contrast to the general flow of public expenditure.

But there was another motive behind these reforms. The courtiers were painfully aware that the Treasury had gradually asserted itself over items of royal spending because of a carefully cultivated belief that courtiers were automatically big spenders and that they could not be expected to produce and enforce substantial savings. Here was evidence which could go a considerable distance to disprove the myth of royal extravagance. The figures showed that, provided the right people were hired to do the job, the Court was perfectly competent to handle its own spending in a prudent manner. It was not to be supposed that the media would take much notice of the Household's achievement; but it would be useful in future dealings with select committees of the House of Commons.

By this time the media were already chasing a different hare: 'and what is more, she doesn't pay a penny tax on any of it'. This story took its place in line beside the exaggerated stories of the Queen's total wealth. The argument about taxation was not immediately easy to counter. There was no long-standing tradition that the monarch did not pay tax. The Queen's father, George VI, was substantially out of pocket as a result of the compensation and other payments which had been awarded to his brother Edward VIII. King George had discussed the problem with the authorities and they concluded that, rather than arguing for an increase in the Civil List with all the parliamentary and public opinion complications, it would be much simpler to reimburse King George, adjusting the tax which had been paid by several of his predecessors. So there was no argument at that time about the tax; but it was offset by repaying to the King through the tax system the monies which he had given to his brother.

This device, while convenient at the time, became distinctly awkward when continued into the Queen's reign. Headlines began to appear about the Queen as a tax dodger, but she had already asked Lord Airlie to investigate the possibilities of her paying tax. When the media storm burst about her, Lord Airlie was almost at the end of this investigation. It was decided to press on the accelerator and the Prime Minister, John Major, announced to the House of Commons that the Queen had voluntarily agreed to pay tax like anyone else. His announcement came two days after the '*annus horribilis*' speech; three months later Lord Airlie gave the press details of the new arrangements in an unprecedented press conference in the picture gallery of St James's Palace.

He spelled out the exemptions from tax which had been agreed with the Treasury, including the exemption from inheritance tax for sovereign-to-sovereign transfers, e.g. from the Queen to the Prince of Wales when he becomes

King. The Prime Minister was initially opposed to the move because he thought that the House of Commons, maybe under a Labour government, would cut away at the exemptions, but the Leader of the Opposition, John Smith, had been consulted and felt able to check what the historian Robert Hardman has called 'some lively tumbril talk from the left'.

Private criticism also came from the Queen Mother, who was anxious about possible harm to her late husband's reputation and was in any case sceptical about several of the Airlie/Peat reforms. The Queen, at all stages, accepted what Lord Airlie was proposing. It was an awkward time for the Queen, as she had already acknowledged in public. The announcement about tax coincided more or less with that of the Prince and Princess of Wales's separation. Lord Airlie admired the steadiness which his Sovereign showed under fire.

More, and almost equally important, changes took place in 1993. For the first time Buckingham Palace was opened to the paying public, with the proceeds helping to fund the restoration of Windsor Castle after the fire, which the Queen had had to finance herself. The new Royal Collection Department was formed to administer these arrangements and to invest the proceeds (£38 million per year) into the maintenance of the Collection. No subsidy of any kind is required for this from the Treasury. This is the story of a quiet revolution, carried out with the blessing of a Queen who is deeply conservative by nature but who tempers this conservatism with a ready acceptance of the influences that have altered the attitudes of her subjects to the changes and chances of modern life.

II

A Time for Rejoicing

At 11.15 a.m. on 22 June 1897 Queen Victoria left Buckingham Palace in a carriage drawn by eight cream-coloured horses to give thanks to God in St Paul's Cathedral for the sixty years of her reign. The crowds were out in force and the applause was deafening. Victoria's tour was devised so as to include the East End and some of the poorest streets in London. The Queen was overcome by emotion: 'How kind,' she said, 'how kind they are.'

On Tuesday, 5 June 2012 Queen Elizabeth left Buckingham Palace to give thanks to God in St Paul's Cathedral for the sixty years of her reign. The crowd was out in force; the applause was continuous and emphatic. It was only almost thirty years since a bitter miners' strike had divided the nation; now the people mustered to thank and give honour to the Queen. There were differences of course between the Jubilee celebrations of Queen Victoria in 1897 and those of Queen Elizabeth in 2012. Victoria's Jubilee was organized by her Colonial Secretary, Joseph Chamberlain. He was determined that the whole event should represent the loyal tribute of the greatest Empire the world had ever seen. The emphasis was on the Raj in India, the brightest jewel in that Empire, and the Queen was escorted to the steps of St Paul's Cathedral by Indian cavalry. A collection of Indian princes attended to do honour to their Empress. Almost as impressive was the assembling of the Queen's descendants, children and grandchildren from every corner of Europe.

For Elizabeth's Diamond Jubilee, the number of escorting troops was much smaller; also reduced was the number of children and grandchildren. In the intervening years, royalty had been banished from Germany, Italy, Russia and Greece. Prince Albert's dream of the royal families of Europe (mainly descended from Victoria and himself) gathered together to keep the peace of Europe had faded. The later dream of Commonwealth prime ministers coming together to forge a common policy to address the problems of the Empire and the world had also vanished. Gathered off the Isle of Wight in 2012 was only a small fraction of the number of warships that had drawn up all those years earlier to salute Victoria. But there was no sense of decay or of indignation in the huge crowd which gathered in the Mall for Elizabeth. The people were in high spirits, glad to take part in a genuinely popular royal occasion. The television cameras carried into the homes of millions around the world the image of a happy people turning away from the problems of the moment, taking a day off to congratulate and salute their happy Queen.

The crowds in 1897 and 2012 did not have to worry about the immediate future of the monarchy. The Queen, on both occasions, could rely on the full support of the Prince of Wales. Charles, newly remarried, could put aside for the moment his earlier personal difficulties. Similarly,

Edward had been back on good terms with his mother, Queen Victoria, and few people in the crowd knew the story of Tranby Croft, when the Prince had been made to give evidence in court after a crony had been accused of cheating at cards. Only in the background were warning voices from the poets. Housman turned to the Shropshire voices singing the National Anthem,

> Oh, God will save her, fear you not;
> Be you the men you've been,
> Get you the sons your fathers got,
> And God will save the Queen.

Kipling sounded a more baleful and more prescient voice:

> Far-called our navies melt away –
> On dune and headland sinks the fire –
> Lo, all our pomp of yesterday
> Is one with Nineveh and Tyre!

Before Victoria came to the throne Britain had tried and failed to keep by force her first Empire in North America. During Elizabeth's reign the second British Empire had dissolved peacefully as colony by colony slipped out of colonial rule into independence, leaving under the Crown only the steady old Dominions, which had gained independence of action while retaining the Queen as their Head of State, and a handful of tiny scattered islands. Elizabeth received the same cheers as had greeted Victoria from a country whose monarchy after two World Wars was even more deeply rooted in the affection of the people.

The House of Windsor had also learned its lessons. The Crown had moved without being seen to do so. Queen Elizabeth was not by nature a reformer, let alone a revolutionary, but she knew she had to move when necessary. If George III had learned that lesson earlier he might have saved the American colonies; if Charles I had learned the lesson in his time, he might have saved his head. To celebrate the past is not to predict the future. What is certain is uncertainty; each monarch brings to the task a set of his or her individual tastes and preoccupations. Our queens have achieved more popularity than our kings, if only because they have the knack for living much longer (Victoria, Elizabeth and indeed Elizabeth I). There will be ups and downs and occasional moments of misgiving; but as an institution the monarchy is deeply rooted in British soil.

12
Church and State

In June 1994, as already recorded, I travelled with the Queen to Normandy to celebrate the fiftieth anniversary of D-Day. At one point in the day I found myself in company with the French Foreign Minister, Alain Juppé, who later became Prime Minister and who was already a personal friend. Our paths then diverged: I went to one of the beaches on which British troops had landed in 1944 and Juppé paid his respects at a monument in honour of the Free French. I met him again later in the day, and I asked him out of curiosity how the British and the French services had varied. He replied at once that he had been surprised by the religious content of the British service that he had attended earlier that day. His surprise was not directed at any doctrinal difference; he was simply startled by the large part that religion had played in our ceremony. The sight of British soldiers joining wholeheartedly in the hymn 'Oh God, Our Help in Ages Past' had no parallel on the French side. The distinction between Church and State in France dated back to the 1789 Revolution; our practice likewise reflected our own history and the coming-together of the English monarch with the Church of England.

The Queen is the Head of the Church of England and the appointment of bishops and deans rests with her, although in practice she acts after receiving the advice of others. This duty is sometimes mixed up in people's mind with the fact that one of the Queen's titles is 'Defender of the Faith'; this title has a quite different history. Henry VIII held on to the title, which Pope Leo X granted him in response to a pamphlet the King wrote asserting the supremacy of the Pope, when he broke away from Rome and brought into being the English Church under his royal control. It is one of the quirks of history that Henry's successors have generally retained this title, which the Pope awarded, and yet have continued to protect themselves by their headship of a Protestant Church of England, which includes a rule excluding Roman Catholics from succeeding to the throne.

This inheritance is important to the Queen as a firm believer in the Christian faith as proclaimed by the Church of England. She took an oath to that effect on her Coronation in June 1953, in which she affirmed in Westminster Abbey the pledge she had given as Princess Elizabeth six years earlier from Cape Town. This undertaking of service throughout her life, 'whether it be long or short', is of crucial importance to her and one of the reasons why she has never accepted the idea of abdication, though the temptations must sometimes have been rather strong. The Coronation embodies the essential character of the English monarchy. As the Bishop of London pointed out in a lecture in June 2013, most of the elements of the 1953 rite were already in place when the Saxon King Edgar was crowned in 973 at Bath: the investiture with ring, sword and crown and the anointing with holy oil, together with the oath of faithful service. As the centuries passed, the outward trappings of the Coronation changed but the essence was the same. George I, our first Hanoverian King, knew so little English that the sense of the service had to be explained to him in Latin. At the Coronation of George III, the sermon was largely inaudible because it was interrupted by the popping of champagne corks in the Lords and Commons. After this came the preposterous efforts of King George IV to stage an event of unrivalled splendour in 1821 and, following the dim days at the end of Victoria's reign, the embellishment of the Coronation service in 1902, 1911 and 1937 took on board the might and splendour of the British Empire. At the same time the architecture of Westminster was in effect rebuilt to accommodate great processions.

Queen Elizabeth's Coronation was memorable even though the British Empire was dissolving around her. The thrones of Europe were for the most part empty, and the monarchs in Holland and Scandinavia who survived had put aside their splendour to suit the austerity of the times. The Bishop of London posed to himself the question 'whether Westminster will soon join Aachen and Rheims as an empty stage inhabited only by ghosts'. However, the nation had rediscovered its taste for pageantry. The Gold State Coach journeyed over the roads of London to Westminster Abbey and the crowds responded cheerfully to the waves of a beautiful young Queen. One generation had passed with the ending of Empire; another generation turned on their new television sets to see glimpses of their country's past but also its future.

The next Coronation is still, we hope, a long way off but already we know that it will follow the same principle; it will preserve the old essence while being brought up to date with the realities of the present. There will be no glitter of Indian cavalry and no loyal ovations from hereditary peers and peeresses. These gaps, made inevitable by history, can be filled by newcomers who have not hitherto been part of a Coronation; but it is certain that there will be a Coronation and that it will be an occasion of joy and thanksgiving complete with bonfires and street parties. The new King will swear the traditional oath. There has been some debate on Prince Charles's remark about taking the title of Defender of Faith; people perhaps fail to notice that the Queen made a similar point when she addressed the assembled bishops at Lambeth in 2012: 'Here at Lambeth Palace we should remind ourselves of the significant position of the Church of England in our nation's life. The concept of our established Church is occasionally misunderstood and, I believe, commonly under-appreciated. Its role is not to defend Anglicanism to the exclusion of other religions. Instead, the Church has a duty to protect the free practice of all faiths in this country.' In recent years I have observed this principle in practice in my job as High Steward of Westminster Abbey. On the main national occasions I have watched the Dean, John Hall, welcome representatives of all Christian faiths to take part in the Abbey, not as strange additions but as partners in the fellowship of Christ.

13
The Sport of Kings and Queens

The most engaging photographs of the Queen are usually taken on the stand of a racecourse. Heedless of other cares, she is fully engaged in the race. There is nothing fixed about her smile on these occasions, and we can almost hear the laughter which lies behind it. The Queen is enjoying her favourite hobby; there is nothing casual about her interest in horse racing, and it is backed up by her formidable memory of the achievements of the horses taking part in the contest before her eyes.

The Queen runs a stable of twenty brood mares looked after by different trainers. John Warren, her Bloodstock Manager and Racing Adviser, is invited each year to Balmoral. There, the Queen and he settle down to the strenuous task: the Queen has to decide which stallions should go with which mares and which horses should be entered for which race in the calendar. This exercise is sheer enjoyment for the Queen, and like most worthwhile pleasures it has to be taken seriously. There is nothing new about the Monarch owning racehorses; they have done so for several generations. What is new is the wholehearted enthusiasm of the Queen for flat racing. This enthusiasm is not shared with Prince Philip, whose interest is in carriage-driving; nor with the Prince of Wales, although that may change as time passes. The Queen Mother was devoted to national hunt racing but her daughter concentrates on the flat.

The Queen does not bet heavily and keeps her sporting ambitions within bounds. The total of twenty brood mares is small beside the much bigger stables of such men as the Aga Khan and Sheikh Mohammed bin Rashid Al Maktoum. The Queen does not aim to compete with them: as her Bloodstock Manager puts it, 'she is interested in the journey, not the prize'. She is glad to win races, though she is still waiting for success in the Derby. Before her jockey gets into the saddle the horse he is riding has undergone many months of selection and training, and it is this process which fascinates the Queen. There is no doubt about her genuine devotion to racing. This is not something contrived for the cameras.

There is one reason for her enthusiasm which is not always realized: racing is a virtually classless sport. This may seem a rash statement given the huge wealth of the leading owners, but in the paddock everyone is treated as equal, jockey, trainer and owner are alike. Admittedly the Queen is different, but on these occasions she mingles happily with the rest of the racing fraternity on equal terms, which she thoroughly enjoys. When the Queen won the Cheltenham Gold Cup she invited all concerned, particularly the Irish jockey, to a banquet of celebration at Windsor and there are still happy memories of that occasion. To escape from official constraints, even for one afternoon spent in congenial company among people unified in their enthusiasm and enjoyment, must come as a welcome refreshment.

14
The Centre Holds

I am sure that the Queen has never summoned a meeting, saying to her staff, 'Today we are going to discuss what reputation I will leave behind: we need to examine the character of my reign.' This is not the way the Queen works any more than did her father before her. The Queen does not believe in sudden decisions taken for public relations purposes. She is, as has been mentioned, by nature conservative, and by instinct leans towards existing practice and convention. The character of her reign has been determined slowly and thoughtfully, decision by decision, as each becomes necessary, which may consecutively form a general pattern. But each decision is taken on its own merits, subject only to her commitment to the service of her people.

One of her first decisions was not consciously taken but handed on from past tradition. She inherited and accepted an annual calendar of events from which she departs only occasionally and reluctantly for practical reasons. Year after year, she spends Christmas at Sandringham and attends a church service on Christmas morning. She hands out the Maundy Money each year in a different cathedral just before Easter. Trooping the Colour precedes Royal Ascot in June, followed by Balmoral for most of the summer, including a stay by the prime minister. One can imagine different monarchs, for example Edward VIII, scrapping this stately procession of events, perhaps substituting a different pattern, perhaps dispensing with the whole concept of a routine calendar as outdated. The present arrangement was worked out by Victoria and Albert to suit their tastes; it continues today despite the invention of television, email and jet planes. The Queen has added to it by inserting her own travel to other countries on state visits and similar inward journeys by foreign guests, who are entertained either at Buckingham Palace or at Windsor. These visits are worked out carefully with the prime minister and the Foreign and Commonwealth Office.

But beyond tradition, the Queen has been guided by the pledge to serve which she gave on her twenty-first birthday in 1947. The words were simple but the years have shown that they were uttered in deep conviction. The fulfilment of that promise has been the story of her life. The anecdotes about Lilibet in her childhood tell the same story – of a serious girl to whom her word was her bond. It was an awesome pledge and few would have blamed her if circumstances had made it impossible to keep. The Queen has kept it in full measure, as validated by her grandson in the Preface to this book. I know from my own experience that it is true.

Sometimes the media seize on a parallel in history and seem determined to make it fit the present facts like the pieces of a baffling jigsaw puzzle. They force the piece this way and that, trying to jam it into the shape required. So it has been with attempts to draw parallels between Elizabeth I and Elizabeth II. The two Queens have the name in common, but nothing else. That has not prevented the press from inventing forced similarities between the two reigns and in this way the myth of a new Elizabethan age was born, one that harks back to the age perhaps most powerfully encapsulated by the first Elizabeth in her speech given in August 1588 at Tilbury to the troops gathered to defend the realm from Spanish invasion:

> I am come [. . .] to live and die amongst you all; to lay down for my God, and for my Kingdom, and my people, my honour and my blood, even in the dust. I know I have the body of a weak and feeble woman; but I have the heart and stomach of a King, and of a King of England too, and think foul scorn that Parma, Spain or any Prince of Europe should dare to invade the borders of my realm.

Of course there is a parallel here, but it is not between Elizabeth I and Elizabeth II: it is between Elizabeth I in 1588 and Winston Churchill in 1940. What the men drawn up at Tilbury heard was their Queen defying the enemies of England; that was enough for them, and it should be enough for us.

'For God's sake, let us sit upon the ground. And tell sad stories of the death of kings'; so Richard II speaks in Shakespeare's play. Such an occupation would be as far removed as possible from the Queen's own inclination. She is a person who focuses on the present, on what needs to be done now or in the near future. She sees little purpose in mulling over the past or indeed peering into a future which is unpredictable. The world around Elizabeth II is full of disorder and suffering, as it has always been, but the future of the British monarchy appears to be as secure as at any time in its history; indeed, if we look back it would be difficult to find a period in which the monarchy was more secure. The succession will pass from the Queen to a Prince of Wales of tested worth and integrity, and thereafter to a grandson who has already shown wisdom beyond his years. The black clouds which seemed to threaten the monarchy thirty years ago have been dispelled, not least by the sure touch of the Queen herself.

The Queen knows that she will be succeeded by someone of different tastes and priorities to her own. Our sadness will be mixed with curiosity about the future and anxiety about the prospects of change. But that anxiety will be much less than at similar moments in the past because of the Queen's example and the reduced scope of the Royal prerogative. Of course, as I have tried to show, there is still plenty of ambiguity in the working of the British constitution; perhaps this would be more kindly called flexibility. There will always be those who want to pin the monarchy down or rather hedge it about with precise definitions designed to cope with every possible turn of events. The trouble with this approach is that we might in our eagerness for certainty provide for every event except the one which actually occurs.

The political neutrality of the Crown lies at the heart of its continuing success. The Queen has shown the way. If she had given in to the irritation which Queen Victoria displayed continuously towards Gladstone, or George III towards most of his ministers, the monarchy might again have been in danger. In the end, within a democracy, the Crown relies on the loyalty of the people. Loyalty is a vague concept which can apply to many human situations. We can be loyal to our parents, to our brothers and sisters, to our employers, to our friends. The loyalty which links us to the Crown is peculiar because it is not based on any family tie or material consideration.

It happens that I have spent most of my working life within sight of Horse Guards where each year in June the ceremony of Trooping the Colour, the annual parade to celebrate the Sovereign's birthday, takes place. Whenever possible I have managed to abandon my desk, whether in the Conservative Research Department, or in the Northern Ireland Office, or in the Home Office, or in my rather grand quarters in the Foreign Office, to watch the last ten or fifteen minutes of the parade. It consists of a complicated series of manoeuvres in slow time and then quick time, carried out in turn by the regiments of the Queen's Foot Guards, dressed in their full scarlet uniform with the traditional bearskin cap and closed by a mounted display by the Household Cavalry. The Queen inspects her Guards as they march past her. Their marching has always been practised in advance and is impeccable, indeed probably the best of its kind in the world; the whole parade is a display of marvellous order and discipline.

As a result of my many years of spectating, I have lodged in my mind a picture of the Queen, erect in her scarlet military tunic, expertly seated side-saddle on a great horse called Burmese, leading her troops year by year up the Mall at the end of the ceremony. Times change and we change with them. The Queen in the scarlet tunic has mutated into an elderly lady in a carriage and the infantry now carry ungainly rifles designed by NATO. No matter, the trees in the Mall look the same, the clapping crowd is the same, the tunes played by the band are familiar and I have happily received my annual reminder of Britain's unique capacity for loyalty, tradition and steadfastness.

Further Reading

Books about the Queen and the royal family pour from the presses every year, so what follows is highly selective. Marion Crawford, nanny to Princesses Elizabeth and Margaret, published *The Little Princesses* (New York: Harcourt, Brace) in 1950 and was ostracized for doing so, though the book was wholly admiring and anodyne by modern standards. The best recent book from inside the royal circle is Margaret Rhodes, *The Final Curtsey* (London: Umbria, 2011). The first serious biography of the Queen was *Majesty: Elizabeth II and the House of Windsor* (London: Hutchinson, 1978) by Robert Lacey, still worth reading. The most authoritative full modern biography is Ben Pimlott, *The Queen: A Biography of Elizabeth II* (London: HarperCollins, 1996). Also enjoyable and insightful are Sarah Bradford, *Elizabeth: A Biography of Her Majesty the Queen* (London: William Heinemann, 1996) and its distillation *Queen Elizabeth: Her Life in Our Times* (London: Penguin, 2012); and Andrew Marr, *The Diamond Queen: Elizabeth II and Her People* (London: Macmillan, 2011), published for the Diamond Jubilee in 2012 and arranged thematically rather than chronologically. The authorized biographies of Queen Elizabeth the Queen Mother (London: Macmillan, 2009) and Lord Mountbatten (London: William Collins, 1985) are by William Shawcross and Philip Ziegler respectively; both give important perspectives on the Queen's life.

Picture Credits

1. Princess Elizabeth with her family in the garden of Royal Lodge, Windsor, 1936 (© Illustrated London News Ltd/Mary Evans)
2. Elizabeth as a 2nd Subaltern in the Auxiliary Territorial Service, April 1945 (© Trustees of the Imperial War Museum, London, TR 2835)
3. Elizabeth before the microphone for her twenty-first birthday speech, Cape Town, 21 April 1947 (© Illustrated London News Ltd/Mary Evans)
4. Princess Elizabeth and Prince Philip, the Duke of Edinburgh, after their wedding ceremony, 20 November 1947 (Daily Mail/Rex Features)
5. Elizabeth greeted at London Airport by Lord Woolton, Anthony Eden, Clement Attlee and Winston Churchill following the death of King George VI, 7 February 1952 (TopFoto)
6. Queen Elizabeth II, Queen Mary and Queen Elizabeth, the Queen Mother at King George VI's funeral, 15 February 1952 (Keystone/HIP/TopFoto)
7. Queen Elizabeth II at her Coronation in Westminster Abbey, 2 June 1953 (PA Photos)
8. Elizabeth II at Buckingham Palace, December 1969 (Joan Williams/Rex Features)
9. Elizabeth II with James Callaghan, Alec Douglas-Home, Margaret Thatcher, Harold Macmillan, Harold Wilson and Edward Heath at 10 Downing Street, December 1985 (PA Photos/TopFoto)
10. Elizabeth II riding her horse Burmese for the final time during Trooping the Colour, June 1986 (AP/PA Photos)

11. Elizabeth II working on her red box of official papers, 1991 (© David Secombe/Camera Press London)

12. Elizabeth II welcomed by Isa bin Salman Al Khalifa, the Emir of Bahrain, during her tour of the Gulf States, 14 February 1979 (Tim Graham/Getty Images)

13. Prince Charles, Elizabeth II and Prince Philip at the decommissioning service for the Royal Yacht *Britannia*, 11 December 1997 (Rex Features)

14. Elizabeth II surveys the damage caused by the fire inside Windsor Castle, 21 November 1992 (Tim Ockenden/PA Photos)

15. The Queen and the Duke of Edinburgh among the well-wishers and floral tributes outside Buckingham Palace on the eve of the funeral of Diana, Princess of Wales, 5 September 1997 (Tony Harris/PA Photos)

16. Elizabeth II watches one of her horses compete in the Veteran Horse class at the Royal Windsor Horse Show, 11 May 2011 (Steve Parsons/PA Photos)

17. Prince Charles pays tribute to Elizabeth II as she joins performers on stage at the end of the Diamond Jubilee Concert at Buckingham Palace, 4 June 2012 (PA Photos/TopFoto)

Acknowledgements

I am most grateful to my agent, Michael Sissons, for introducing me to Penguin, and to my thorough but kindly editor there, Stuart Proffitt. I am, in addition, particularly grateful to Lords Fellowes, Janvrin and Luce, Lady Susan Hussey, and Mr John Warren, the Queen's Bloodstock Manager. Also, for their invaluable help, Terri Good, Chloe Campbell, Ed Young, Linden Lawson, Olga Davies, Estelle Millard, Ben Sinyor, Cecilia Mackay and Anna Hervé.

Index